101 Rules of Real Estate Investing

– Essential Keys to Unlocking Your First $1,000,000 –

Matt Merdian and Laurence Samuels

VISIT

WWW.101RULES.COM

As a thank you for purchasing this book we invite you to visit our website www.101rules.com where you will find endless resources to help you achieve your business goals and dreams.

Also Available: Real Estate and Tax Deed Deed Investing

All the information you need to become a successful real estate real estate investor!

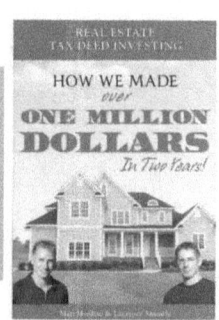

Limit of Liability / Disclaimer of NO warranty:

The authors and publishers are not real estate agents, attorneys, or financial advisors.

Revisions and editing by Monica Bedi
Additional editing provided by Judy Samuels
This book is printed in the United States of America.

Books are available for quantity discounts for sales, promotions, and educational purposes. Please email our sales department at info@ londonmeridian.com for more information.

Published by London Meridian Publishing LLC
ISBN: 1481174487
ISBN 13:   9781481174480

PREFACE

Many people ask us why we wrote *101 Rules of Real Estate Investing*. Simply answered, we wrote it for you. We wrote this book for the person who dreams of quitting the drudgery of the 9 to 5 job they dislike. We wrote it for the person who has always been interested in becoming a real estate investor but afraid to take that first step. We wrote it for the person who has already purchased a few investment homes but wants to make sure they are on the right track.

In the early stages of our real estate careers, we found most people unwilling to share information about the do's and don'ts of investing. We vowed that if we were ever to be successful, we would always share this information with others.

Our first book, *Real Estate Tax Deed Investing, How we made over One Million Dollars in Two Years!* was written to provide a wealth of information about Real Estate Tax Deed investing. We are proud of the book and its contents. Since then we have been asked by multiple investors to expand our publications to include more general topics such as managing rental properties and dealing with difficult contractors. These topics and many more are covered in *101 Rules of Real Estate Investing*.

Real Estate Investing is so much more than just buying, fixing and selling houses. Investing is a sum of many parts including interaction, organization and making smart decisions.

101 Rules of Real Estate Investing offers you information you may have never considered such as life lessons and pitfall avoidance. When applied correctly, these rules will potentially save you tens of thousands of dollars, not to mention time and frustration.

We hope our experiences and stories will light the pathway so you can reach your goals and dreams, whatever they may be.

-Matt and Laurence

BEFORE YOU READ ON
SIGN UP TO WIN A FREE COACHING SESSION VALUED AT $150

It is important you do this BEFORE you read this book!

www.101rules.com/coaching

CONTENTS

CREATING YOUR TEAM

LEGAL AND PROTECTION

CONTRACTS

CONTRACTORS

ACCOUNTING

LOCATION, LOCATION, LOCATION...

NEGOTIATING

SALES AND MARKETING

CREATING
YOUR TEAM

With Strength in Numbers, 2+2 can Equal 5

Welcome to your new world of real estate and congratulations for taking steps towards you making your first million! This journey is not a race and will not happen overnight. Becoming a successful real estate investor takes passion, vision, hard work, dedication, knowledge, tenacity, and desire. This journey will test your will and ability to deal with complex situations. Each challenge you face will have multiple solutions and it is up to you to find the best one.

How will you choose to set out on this journey? Is it better to take this journey alone, with a business partner or with a larger group? The correct decision will lay the foundation for your success.

When forming our business, we chose to work together as a two-person partnership. We discovered that the arduous journey is best traveled with a business partner. A business partner should be someone you know, trust, respect, shares similar goals with, and someone you can communicate openly and easily with.

Starting a business can be daunting at times and there is a sense of comfort knowing that you are not alone. Complicated decisions and problems with unobvious solutions will challenge you on your quest to make your first million dollars.

When you are faced with a problem, it is far easier for two people to find solutions. That is not to say you aren't capable of problem solving on your own, but many more solutions and ideas can be created by two people. Why is this? One person's solutions may come as a result of their knowledge and experience. When we problem solve, one of us likes to play Devil's Advocate. On our own, it is more difficult to sit on both sides of the fence. When two or more people join together to pool their knowledge and experiences, that power is multiplied and solutions and ideas flow more easily. It is also more difficult to make tough decisions when you are making them alone. Those decisions might be delayed through procrastination. When you have someone else to help you and hold you accountable, tough decisions can be made in a timely manner.

For example, we purchased a two-bedroom, one-bathroom home that needed some major repairs. The property was one hour's drive away from our office. After acquiring the property we realized that in order to fix the house into saleable condition, the repairs were going to cost far more than we had anticipated.

The property was located in an area where rental rates were high and a nice cash flow could be generated which presented us with a dilemma. Should we spend the extra money on the property in order to resell or rent the property in its current condition to start receiving immediate cash flow? There were many pros and cons to both decisions. One of us was in favor of renting the property as-is, resulting in a smaller short-term income. The other was in favor of renovating, selling and cashing out. This renovation route would require more money and work before any financial returns would be seen. We were both very set on what we thought was the best decision.

After much discussion we decided to place rental ads for our house in local newspapers and on websites. As the calls came in we spoke with the potential renters and explained the property would be available in 30-45 days. We generated a lead list of 15 rental applicants, and then attended meetings at local real estate investment clubs and spoke with investors. Since we were able to generate a great list of potential renters, we quickly found an investor to purchase the house therefore reducing our selling time.

If either one of us had made the decision individually, a different path would have been chosen yielding different results. Working together enabled us to make the best decision. We have many friends that chose to start their real estate businesses alone but for us a partnership was the right choice. Whichever decision you make, make sure it is one that is comfortable for you and you will be well on your way to unlocking your first million!

Surround Yourself with People More Successful than You

Being an entrepreneur is very exciting but it will force you to make some tough, life changing decisions. We try to model ourselves on the people we spend most time with.

Prior to working in the real estate business, we both worked in other industries and continued to maintain friendships with co-workers. While we appreciated these friendships, we noticed some of the people we spent a lot of our time with were not progressing in their lives; some of them were not working at all. There came a point where a tough decision had to be made. Were we to maintain these friendships and perhaps be held back, or was it time to find alternative friends and mentors? The choice was an obvious but difficult one to make. We discovered that in order to be successful in business, we needed to spend time with people that were positive minded and more successful than ourselves.

We were able to forge friendships and working relationships with business professionals who pushed us to work smarter and harder. Some of our existing friends did not think this way, as they were content to glide through life at a mediocre pace, striving for no more than a week-to-week paycheck from an employer.

As we began to spend time with people more successful than ourselves, we discovered our business grew at a faster rate. These people were kind enough to give us ideas and advice regarding situations they had also experienced themselves. We love all of our old friends but if we had approached them with such situations, they would not have had any idea of how to help or advise us.

Spend more time with people who you would like to mirror. You will that find over time, their characteristics will adhere to you and these relationships will help you grow and succeed much faster within your own business.

Find a Mortgage Broker Who Works for You!

Throughout our 101 Rules of Real Estate we advise a common theme of 'building your team wisely'. Pick your team members very carefully as these members not only work for *you* but also represent *you*.

Not all mortgage brokers are made equal! Do not hire someone just because they are your best buddy or family friend! Hire a professional with a proven track record of loan completions and choose someone who writes mortgages for a living rather than as part time income.

Your mortgage broker is a key player on your team. Finding the correct mortgage broker goes much deeper than finding someone who can offer you the lowest interest rate. An experienced broker knows which types of loans he can realistically approve for you. The last thing you want is for some cowboy broker wasting weeks of your time on a loan application that never has a chance of being approved. It happens all the time as some brokers are compensated based on the amount of applications they process

Great mortgage brokers understand their mortgage products inside and out and know exactly what the banks are looking for in order to get you approved quickly.

Our main mortgage broker is Rich Condon and is an expert in the field. Here is what Rich he had to say:

"Leveraging other people's money is an effective way to build an income generating real estate portfolio, now more than ever with rates at historic lows. Having a knowledgeable lending partner that shares your vision is essential to your success. The right financing can be the bridge to your success in real estate."

For more recommendations on mortgage brokers visit www.101rules.com/tools

Property Appraisers can be Your Best Friends!

To sell a property you need to do the following math:

Buy + repair + market + real estate agent + buyer + bank + appraiser = SOLD

Some people believe they have no influence over the property appraiser, but this is simply untrue. You can have a great deal of influence.

Most banks use the same appraisers over and over again because they have built up a trusting relationship with them. We LOVE property appraisers and treat them with politeness and respect. Why? Because assuming everyone else has done their job properly and all the buyers' paperwork has been completed correctly, the appraiser is one of the final hurdles before a real estate transaction closes. The appraiser can make or break your deal.

The bank looks to their appraisers to give the seal of approval on a piece of real estate to show that it is actually worth the money the buyer is paying for it! In the real estate boom days when computers were automatically approving loans, some appraisals weren't worth the paper they were written on. Properties were being over-valued and the appraisals seemed to be after thoughts.

Post 2007, banks seem to have over compensated with the strictness of loan approvals and would now like you to think they are there to help protect the consumer. Really this is all smoke and mirrors and these strict guidelines are in place to protect the banks! Obviously the banks do not want to lend money on a property that is worth less than the loan amount, risking the property becoming upside-down in value if loan payments are not made.

As an investor, your goal is to sell your properties for the maximum amounts possible. Sales transactions almost always involve a bank so an appraiser will be involved.

How can you use the appraiser to your benefit? You can provide the appraiser with current information about sold homes in the area. It is your job and your real estate agent's job to know this information. Turn the appraiser into your best friend and convey as much information to him as possible. The time and effort spent may help solidify your sales price. Some investors we know look upon appraisers as the evil enemy sent by the bank to knock down the sales price. Most of the time, this simply is not true as appraisers generally want all parties to be happy.

Banks commonly use the same appraiser on a recurring basis. The more you become involved in real estate investing, the more chance you have of dealing with the same appraisers, especially in smaller towns or cities. The better you treat the bank appraisers, the smoother your selling transactions will become!

On the reverse side, we have used our relationships with appraisers to purchase a property for less than the price we offered. Our very first property that we purchased through our real estate agent is a perfect example. This fixer-upper house needed much work but it was located in a great area of downtown Orlando. We assessed the property, put in an offer and went back and forth with the bank before we agreed upon a price. But we did not stop there.

When we met with the bank's appraiser, we pointed out all the issues with the house and showed him a print-out containing comparable values of other perfect condition homes in the area. Our purpose for doing this was to try to drive the bank's price down. This deal was going to be made with cash as no financing was available due to the poor condition of the home and the bank was anxious to sell the property as soon as possible. To our chagrin, the appraisal came back a little under our proposed offer. Pat then reduced our offer even further below the bank's appraisal price and the bank accepted it!

The couple of extra hours you spend with the appraiser can definitely make a difference. Provide the appraiser with as much information as possible as this can really help you with your transactions.

Promote Full Honesty, Openness, and Acceptance of Your Business Partner's Opinions

Any time money, emotions, friends, business partners, and decisions are involved, conflict can arise.

You should always be honest about what is happening and what can happen. Always be truthful no matter what situation you find yourself in. Do not hide the possible outcomes resulting from the decisions you are making just because you are afraid of upsetting someone. Not all decisions are good and they may lead to financial losses or other downsides. This is part of being an entrepreneur.

Openness is the key to having healthy conversations with your business partner, especially in regards to sensitive issues. The more straightforward you are with the people you do business with, the more open they will be to your ideas and vice versa.

We have been in situations where we held back the severity of a complicated issue due to concern of how the news would be taken. After things went sour, the situation worsened causing serious issues between our business associate and us.

One time, we partnered with a business associate to purchase a piece of land totaling five acres. Before purchasing, we hired an engineer to study the land and report any potential hazards. The engineer informed us there was a slight chance the land may be home to an endangered species of gopher turtles. If there was any evidence of these turtles, an environmental company would have to be hired to relocate the turtles at considerable cost. We mistakenly decided to risk proceeding forward with the land purchase as we thought finding these turtles would be highly unlikely.

During the permitting phase, the city required us to dig test holes on the land to ensure it was gopher turtle free. After digging the first hole, we found several turtle eggs and were informed we would need to find and remove the turtles at a cost of $10,000. Our business associate was very upset that we had not informed him of this matter prior to purchasing the land. It wasn't that we were trying to hide anything from him; we just did not see the need to alarm him since we assumed the land was turtle free.

If we had been open and honest about the situation, our associate could have helped find an alternative solution. We should have remembered that being in a partnership means partners through the good AND the bad news!

Remember to be honest, open-minded, and take every suggestion and solution you are offered seriously. Sometimes suggestions may sound flat out crazy but keep in mind the person giving you the suggestion may be trying to contribute and achieve the same goals as you are. Just because you are listening to a suggestion doesn't mean that it has to be implemented. Acceptance and implementation are two different things. We have learned that the more open we are to other people's ideas, the more solutions we find.

Value the opinions of others by being honest, open, and accepting. These simple suggestions will provide you with a healthier relationship with your business partners!

Happy Neighbors = Trouble-Free Projects

Construction projects are messy affairs and no matter how careful you and your subcontractors are, there is inevitably going to be some debris and dirt.

Some of our construction projects have been particularly messy but there was one particular project that stands out. We purchased a house at auction that desperately needed a garage due to the lack of interior storage space.

When we work on houses we try to clean up all work areas at the end of every day otherwise the mess accumulates and before you know it, you are knee deep in a construction disaster zone. Debris such as nails and metal splinters can be a real safety issue.

During the construction of the garage, we noticed the subcontractors were being rather lazy with their cleanup efforts. We tried to explain the importance of cleanliness to the subcontractors and while their efforts to improve were admirable, they still managed to leave a considerable mess each day.

One afternoon, while at the house with a potential buyer, an angry neighbor named George knocked on the front door. George explained that he had grown tired of living next door to a construction zone and the previous day, his wife had run over several nails destroying two of her tires. We apologized to George and offered to pay for the tires which he thanked us for. We also provided him with two gift cards to his favorite restaurant as a token of our appreciation for his patience during construction. We decided it would be best to do the same for the neighbors on the other side of the house.

Before we begin a construction project, we now knock on our neighbors' doors and explain our plans and give them gift cards. It helps keep the peace during a trying time. We recommend you do the same, as it will save you many neighborly headaches.

Proprietary Fund Lending is Banking's Best Secret

Some large corporate banks care little about their customers, even pulling fast moves such as charging monthly fees for ATM cards. When we parted ways with our large corporate bank, we decided to switch to smaller community banks and began meeting the executives who ran them. We gained so much information from these people and found that they truly shared and valued our entrepreneurial spirit.

Some of these bank executives were successful real estate investors themselves and wanted to help us on our journey to success. This was very important to us because these bankers understood that the more successful we became, the more business we could send their way. This was quite the opposite from the treatment we received from the giant corporate banks.

Most banks that lend you money will resell these loans to other financial institutions, so it is purely a numbers game to them. There is no personal involvement and some banks have no vested interest in your success.

During our many conversations with smaller sized bank presidents, many of them spoke of Proprietary Funds. Proprietary Funds are monies the bank lends which they either own or have acquired from private investors. This type of fund or loan is not resold on the open market so the bank has a vested interest in whoever borrows money from this fund. Why is that important? It means the bank believes in your business and your product! In some cases it is much easier to qualify for a Proprietary Fund loan than a regular business loan.

If you have a track record of making smart decisions and can show a history of some profit making, then this type of funding is one you should seek out for new ventures.

When you find your next deal, try to work with a banker who understands your business and can provide access to Proprietary Funds.

Never Throw Away Phone Numbers or Contacts

One day at a Tax Deed Auction, we purchased a great property located in Deltona, Florida. The property was a typical three-bedroom, two-bathroom house with a two-car garage. We love these types of properties because they are easy to sell for a profit.

The property was in decent shape but there were some issues in the bathroom. The grout had not been sealed correctly so the tiled shower walls and shower pan had disintegrated due to water damage. The shower controls were also leaking prompting us to call our plumber.

Unfortunately our regular plumber was working on a large commercial project and could not spare a worker. We contacted our other plumbers but they were also too busy to help.

With few other options available we decided to try Craigslist. If you have ever used Craigslist to hire help then you will know how inconsistent it can be. After calling 10 plumbers and leaving 10 messages, only two called us back. With little background information to go, we chose a plumber and asked him to meet us at the house a couple hours later.

When we first met the plumber named Rob, he looked somewhat familiar but we were preoccupied with other things so we did not pay him much attention. About an hour into the project we remembered where we had fired Rob the plumber from another job two years ago! The job he was working on required a permit, which Rob told us he had obtained prior to starting. A few days later, a city inspector made a surprise visit, shut down our jobsite and fined us for not pulling a permit. Rob lied to us about pulling the permit which cost us dearly so he was fired immediately.

If we had kept Rob's contact details we would have known not to hire him before we even picked up the phone. We reminded Rob of the previous fiasco and once again he was terminated.

You may be wondering why we didn't give Rob a second chance and let him finish the job? The answer is we do not support contractors who lie and fail to meet their obligations.

If we had kept the names and numbers of the people we had bad experiences with, this would have never have happened. Nowadays we keep a file with notes on every contractor we hire, both good and bad, and always keep it nearby when hiring out jobs.

This file is especially useful when people ask us for references. We are able to share our experiences with other investors and help prevent them from hiring problematic contractors.

Keeping all information on previously hired contractors has allowed us to create a special place in our file named the 'Red Zone'. This is reserved for contractors who have stolen from us. Several years ago we hired an electrician for a small inexpensive job. One of our long time employees told us he saw the electrician's workers helping themselves to some of our power tools. After discussing this with the electrician we were shocked to hear that it was no surprise to him that some of the laborers had stolen our equipment. It sounded as if this had happened before on his other job sites.

The electrician's work was completed satisfactorily and on time, but his laborers denied the theft and essentially ruined the chances of us ever hiring them again.

While we have focused on the negative outcomes, there are plenty of positive reasons to keep the contacts of people, even if you think you may never do business with them again. Old contacts that may seem useless now often come back into your life years later so do not dispose of the information. Print out your contact list in case your computer hard drive fails and always back up your phone's contacts in case you lose it.

Use Referrals to Locate Distressed Property

We cannot stress how important referrals are in the real estate business. Some days our phone rings off the hook with people offering us deals on distressed homes they saw while driving through a neighborhood. We have a large network of people who we pay for such leads.

So where do we find our referrals? Referrals can come from absolutely anyone, but our favorites are:

> Service technicians
> Air conditioning repairman
> Pool cleaners
> Landscape maintenance
> Roofers
> Property managers
> Handymen
> Plumbers

We probably get more referrals from air conditioning (or a/c) repairmen than any other source. Why? We live in Florida and you cannot live in Florida without a/c. If you are down on your luck and out of cash, you could probably do without a/c for a while but eventually when the summer arrives, the heat will catch up with you and you will be making a call to your local a/c company.

If someone's a/c unit has deteriorated due to lack of maintenance, there is a good chance the house has other areas that have been neglected and these types of homes are ones investors like to target. Even if you live in a cold climate, the same rings true for homeowners who have neglected their heating systems.

Sandeep is our favorite air conditioning repairman as he is always giving us leads. One day he was working on a rental house in a great neighborhood and began chatting to the landlord about how the previous tenants had completely destroyed the air conditioning unit. We saw pictures and couldn't believe how badly the unit was destroyed. It turned out that this was the landlord's third eviction in only a year and he was fed up. He had stopped caring for the house and let it go into disrepair.

The landlord's most recent unsavory tenants stole his exterior air conditioning unit after they vacated the property. This was an expensive loss for the landlord. While most of his problems could have been cured by proper tenant screening and background checks, this was the landlord's last straw and he was desperate to be rid of the home.

Sandeep called us immediately and told us of the situation. We were able to negotiate a great deal on the landlord's house and we paid a nice referral fee to Sandeep. Referrals on distressed properties are goldmines so never overlook them!

One of our other favorite types of referrals is from people who deliver telephone books and newspapers. These people see hundreds of houses on their daily work route and are more than happy to pass information along to us for a referral fee.

We have an investor friend named Christine who prior to becoming a real estate investor, struggled to raise three children as a single parent. Now a seasoned investor, Christine has never purchased any of her properties from a real estate agent or a classified ad - they have all come from referrals. Her biggest lead generator was a teenage boy who delivered phonebooks after school. He would see For Sale signs on distressed properties during his delivery routes and report back to Christine. She would then visit the properties and evaluate them. Christine ended up purchasing six rental properties in this manner and compensated the teenager for his leads.

You can never have enough people watching for real estate deals. Always make sure you compensate them well if you purchase a property they refer to you.

Find a Real Estate Agent to List MLS Properties for Lower Commissions

6.0%... The dreaded six percent... $6000 for every $100,000 goes to real estate agent when you sell a piece of real estate. $6000 is a great deal of money, especially when we are trying to run a business that counts on every penny to be profitable.

We love our real estate agent Pat Glenn and he certainly deserves every dollar he earns but we are the investors with money at risk so we have to minimize our expenses as much as possible. Generally speaking, an agent's risk is minimal involving only time and some fixed cost marketing expenses.

The relationship we have with Pat is a close one. He knows details about us including our finances, investments and goals. Since we only use Pat and provide him with recurring properties to sell, we always ask him for a discount on commissions. Pat knows we will always let him market and sell our real estate. Our loyalty to Pat gives us many advantages as he provides us with inside details about the market, potential deals, and a list of buyers looking for specific items.

Finding a great real estate agent like Pat is not always easy but there is a Pat in every town and city; you just have to find him. Many real estate agents jump in and out of the business when the market changes. Find someone who has been in the business for a long time and avoid the inexperienced agents. Experience, dedication, and knowledge should be a given. Find an agent who will not only market your properties, but also help you make smart buying decisions. After our third transaction with Pat, we struck a deal for him to market all of our properties for a discounted commission rate, resulting in us saving large sums of money.

Creating a great relationship with an agent like Pat will not only save you money, but also provide you with a wealth of expert information on the geographical areas you are targeting. Without an agent's input you may make good decisions, but with his input you can make GREAT decisions.

Guide the Inspectors and Create a Friend, Not a Foe

Inspections can be intimidating. Why? Because building inspectors can approve or reject your work in progress and even delay your certificate of occupancy (CO). Whether it's a remodel or a new construction home you will run into these inspectors at some point.

Several of our business associates have become consumed by these inspections. Much of their time and energy has been wasted worrying about the outcome of these inspections. Though these are important, if your contractor has done his job properly, your inspections will be approved... eventually!

These inspectors have good and bad days like you and us. We try to make sure that their experience with us is a pleasant one. We have been on other people's job sites where we see the building site owner arguing with the inspector about this and that – heightening the inspector's frustrations. This is a great example of what NOT to do.

When planning for an inspection appointment, first find out his or her name before they arrive. Usually the county or city knows which inspector will be visiting you. Second, know EXACTLY what it is the inspector is looking for. For example: If you have a plumbing inspector checking new pipes that have been installed in a newly constructed home, generally the inspector will be looking to see if the pipes have passed a pressure test, and that the rake or degree of angle is correct on waste pipes. Make sure you are prepared for what the inspector is looking for and be ready and able to FIX any potential issues on the spot.

We had a project where we were building a 5000 square foot valued at over $1 million home. This building process involved many inspections including electrical. This house being so large required a 400-amp electrical service (this was two to four times larger than a standard home due to the size of the house and the amount of circuits needed).

The electrical inspector's name was John who was a nice man but could also be a stickler if he wanted to be. Our first meeting with John was when he came over to inspect our underground and temporary power supplies.

We asked John what his pet peeves were to which he replied, "Gum on my shoe." What? Our next question was a little specific:

"John, what are your pet peeves about inspecting houses?"

He laughed a little and said, "Builders think they know more than us inspectors… they don't. I inspect more homes and commercial buildings than any one builder will ever step foot in. If they would just do their job right the first time, I wouldn't deny their inspection and we would all be happy! It's the little things like making sure all the electrical wiring drill holes they make in the studs are filled in. It takes almost no time to do but it's an easy reason for a denial. Then I have to come back out again and waste my time away from my family 'cuz someone was lazy."

John did not want to be a stickler for detail; he just wanted to do his job quickly and get home to his wife and kids. With this in mind we were well prepared when he returned for our final inspection.

We asked John if it was alright if we followed him during the inspection in case something had been missed. Before the inspection we pointed out that we had asked the workers to fill all the electrical wiring drill holes but that we had a couple extra cans of the filler just in case they had missed any. Sure enough John did find three drill holes that were not filled in so we fixed them on the spot.

We received the 'Pass' marking on our inspection marking permit and celebrated. John laughed after we said, "Hey John it's a win for everyone, we got a pass, and you didn't get any gum on your shoes!"

Partnerships: You Had Better Have a Good Exit Strategy

Business partnerships can be extremely beneficial. We speak from experience as we enter our second decade as business partners. Not all partnerships run smoothly; we have seen many fail due to a variety of reasons. Sometimes these reasons are due to life changing circumstances.

When we first met Joe and Tom, they had been investing in real estate together for three years and had acquired 10 rental properties.

One day, Tom's wife Karen received some unfortunate news regarding the health of her mother who lived overseas. Since the illness was life-threatening, Karen decided she should move in with her mother to assist her during this difficult time. The overseas move meant Tom would be forced to leave his job in the United States.

In order to complete the move, Tom and Karen needed some financial cushioning. Tom explained to Joe (his business partner) that in order to obtain enough money to move overseas, Tom would need to sell his share of their rental properties. The problem was that Joe did not have access to the money required to buy Tom's share. To make matters worse, the real estate market was in decline and Joe was not sure if they would be able to sell their rental properties before Tom needed to move.

Joe decided he would try to find and an investor to buy Tom's share of the business. In the meantime Karen's mother's health was rapidly deteriorating so Tom and Karen quickly packed up their belongings and placed their house up for sale. Two weeks later despite being alarmingly low on funds, Tom and Karen moved overseas. Joe struggled to find an investor to buy out Tom and decided his only option was to attempt to refinance the 10 rental properties himself.

This option proved to be difficult because they Joe and Tom had qualified for the loans together. Their once firm friendship/partnership began to fall apart as Tom and Joe placed blame on one another for the bad situation. Even though neither person was to blame, a lack of an exit strategy had placed them in this position.

Tom and Joe eventually had to hire a real estate attorney to help mediate between them. Emotions ran high and financially and Tom was close to ruin. The attorney mapped out a plan to liquidate key properties and refinance the others. Two properties were sold while the rest were split equally into separate names giving Tom the passive income he needed to survive overseas.

It was a tough predicament Tom and Joe had placed themselves in as they discovered how difficult it is to quickly liquidate long term assets without taking a financial hit.

Tom explained to us that us he was down to his last $300 when he received his first income payment from his rental properties and that neither he nor Joe had considered an exit strategy for the business.

Exit strategy conversations within partnerships are vital. You should have one whether you own one rental or 100. These types of questions will help you prepare for the unexpected:

What if you cannot sell the property?

Are you willing to rent the property for income?

What liquidation price are you willing to accept?

How long will you wait to consider a liquidation price?

If there is an emergency and one partner needs money right away, what are your options?

If you are considering partnering up with someone, make sure you have a clearly written exit strategy agreement. Sometimes these strategies can take months or even years to execute so keep that in mind. While Joe and Tom's story sounds extreme, situations like this happen frequently. Life is full of surprises, good and bad.

LEGAL AND PROTECTION

Why You Must Protect Your Business...

Placing your business into the form of a C Corporation, S Corporation, or Limited Liability Company (LLC) does not completely relieve you of liability but if formed correctly, a corporation can help limit your liability should a nasty incident occur.

Since laws are constantly changing, we cannot possibly go over all the ins and outs of forming a corporation. Consult your attorney and accountant to choose the correct path. We originally chose to operate as an S Corp, and then later converted to an LLC.

For each major project we form a new LLC so the liability is limited to that single project. For instance, if we create ABC LLC and we get sued, it does not affect any of our projects outside of that LLC because they are separate entities. Should you become involved in a lawsuit, having limited liability is crucial.

You always want to protect yourself, your family, and your finances at all costs. Corporations over-shadow personal liability if formed and operated correctly. They can protect your personal finances should someone try to sue you for your personal assets such as your primary residence or personal savings.

In the case you are sued, it is not impossible for an opposing party to prove personal liability, but it is much more difficult. Just forming the LLC or corporation is not enough. You must follow the laws associated with operating the corporation. For example:

You cannot co-mingle personal and business funds.

You must keep separate bank accounts and accounting for personal and business use.

Loans should be applied for under a business entity.

Directors meetings must take place annually and annual reports must be filed with the appropriate agencies.

Laws change constantly, so always consult a knowledgeable lawyer and accountant to ensure you form and operate your corporation correctly.

Carry a Limited Liability Insurance Policy

Beware, we live in the "sue happy" society and it is only going to get worse. Have you seen how many lawyers' commercials there are on TV now? It is alarming. There are too many people that see using our court system as a get rich quick scheme so you had better make sure you are protected.

Insurance companies sell many types of insurance: car, rental, home, etc. One type that often gets overlooked is General Liability also known as an Umbrella Policy.

Most of these Umbrella policies offer upwards of $1,000,000 of coverage for just a few hundred dollars per year. While $1,000,000 may sound like a huge amount of money, nowadays it is usual to see law suits in the several million dollar range.

Liability insurance can cover many things such as death, dismemberment, injury, etc. A tenant, a tenant's guest, and even a burglar can sue you. Anyone can sue anyone for any reason and even if it doesn't hold up in court, you still need liability coverage!

A tenant could accidentally slip and fall and want to seek damages. If they are entitled to a settlement, that money has to come from somewhere. A General Liability Policy will help cover your potential loss. It is important to remember that this type of insurance is very different from Home Owner's Insurance. General Liability policies can cover you in many different circumstances while Home Owners Insurance is much more specific.

This rule is probably one of the most overlooked rules but one of the most necessary rules in Real Estate. Do not take this advice for granted…buy plenty of insurance.

The amount you need will be decided on many factors:

How much money do you have to lose?

How much money does your business have to lose?

How much debt do you have?

Our investor friend Richard always carried plenty of insurance and this was something he was particularly proud of. His insurance covered him for auto, health and property. One day Richard received a phone call from a contractor who had been working for him on an apartment complex renovation. After the job was completed, the contractor was walking to his car when he tripped on a loose piece of sidewalk. Falling caused the contractor to break his left ankle and he was immediately driven to the hospital. The subcontractor told Richard not to worry about the injury.

Richard did not think twice about the situation until he received an attorney's letter in the mail four weeks later. The letter stated that the Richard's insurance should cover the medical and lost wages costs because the injury occurred on his property. Richard could not believe that the subcontractor was suing him so he was forced to hire an attorney to defend the case.

This situation dragged on for months and Richard racked up thousands of dollars in legal fees. The subcontractor was intent on collecting as much money as possible and was not interested in settling out of court. Court cases like this present many problems but whether Richard liked it or not, he would have to defend himself.

Even though Richard had purchased multiple types of insurance coverage, he missed one important piece of the puzzle-**liability insurance**. If Richard had a liability policy, it may well have covered him in this situation. After almost a year, Richard found himself in court listening as the judge passed a verdict in favor of the subcontractor along with a judgment of $75,000 plus court costs and legal fees. This was an expensive lesson for Richard to learn.

It is inevitable that one day someone will sue you so make sure you are covered by an umbrella liability insurance policy. These policies are inexpensive and will provide you with piece of mind.

Always Purchase Homeowners Insurance on Every Property

Protecting your real estate investment should be your number one priority. Homeowners insurance is relatively cheap to purchase, especially when taking into consideration what you could lose if you do not carry it if disaster strikes.

What if a fire occurs in your property or there is a natural disaster such as a flood or a hurricane? What if your rental property is vandalized during renovation? All of these possibilities make for great reasons to keep your home insurance current with high coverage limits. Most policies will cover most situations but be sure to check with your insurance agent as some States offer separate policies for tornados or hurricanes, and separate flood zone riders if your property is located near water.

We once purchased a home at a Tax Deed auction and were making arrangements to renovate it when disaster struck in the form of a category five hurricane. Some properties in the neighborhood were completely destroyed while others remained untouched. Many roofs had tattered blue tarps hanging from them and some roofs were even pierced by flying light poles. The devastation left in the wake of the hurricane was frightening.

Thankfully our investment property was not destroyed but it did sustain damage to the roof, air conditioning unit, fence, shed, and carport. The repairs totaled more than $12,000, which thankfully were covered by the insurance (less a moderate deductible). Many people think we are too regimented about insurance and tend to carry too much but we think otherwise. Three weeks after the storm, we received an insurance check and immediately began renovation and repair work on our investment house. Being overly insured allowed us to complete the repairs and place the house under contract six months after purchase for a sizable profit. If the home had not been adequately insured, we would have barely broke even.

Always carry plenty of homeowners insurance, as you never know when the perfect storm might strike.

Question: What's the Difference Between a Lawyer and a Herd of Buffalo?

Answer: The Lawyer Charges More.

We bet you can think of a great lawyer joke or two but in real estate, love them or hate them; you will want a good lawyer on your side. Hopefully, you will never need the services of a lawyer, but there is a business saying that goes, "If you haven't been sued, you aren't successful."

Creating a relationship with a lawyer you feel comfortable with is essential to becoming a successful real estate investor. Whether you are renting, buying, selling, etc, if you are involved in multiple deals on a yearly basis, it is to your advantage to have an attorney to call on should problems arise.

In today's society, people sue first and ask questions later. The simplest misunderstanding or wording in a contract can quickly turn into a lawsuit. Simply closing your eyes and hoping a lawsuit never happens is not realistic. You do not necessarily need to retain an attorney but make sure you have access to one if needed. Maybe you have a family friend who practices law and can offer some advice, thus avoiding a trip to court (or avoid being taken to court too!).

So how do you find the right attorney? Talk to people that you have professional relationships with such as your real estate agent or insurance agent. Most of these people will have an attorney they work with or will know of someone. There are many different types of lawyers so be sure to choose one has been practicing for more than 10 years and who specializes in Real Estate law.

Our attorney specifically deals with closings and contract law and is able to foresee any potential problems in our contracts. We turn to our attorney for advice and guidance many times a year and sleep better at night! Try to avoid litigation at all costs. If you have the right lawyer who is truly working for you, he will make sure you stay out of the courtroom.

Retain a Lawyer for Both Contract Law and Litigation

Each type of lawyer has their own fields that they specialize in. As we mentioned previously, our lawyer specializes in contract law, which is extremely valuable to us. By having him them review our contracts, we rest easy knowing our contracts are well written.

If you find yourself involved in a contract dispute that cannot be resolved, you may need a lawyer who specializes in litigation (a trial lawyer). Litigation usually occurs when one of the contracted parties fails to abide by the terms or fails to perform and or meet obligations. Most real estate contracts use mediation (an unbiased third party) to help resolve issues. But there are times when mediation cannot be used so we recommend that you are prepared.

Not all lawyers who specialize in business and real estate contracts are experienced litigators. These types of lawyers are best used to help write and review contracts and can help with out of court disputes by suggesting compromises or mediation. If the issues escalate past the point of mediation, some contract lawyers will refer you to a trial lawyer to litigate.

We find it is wise to be prepared in advance should a situation ever occur. If you wait until something happens, you may find you don't have enough time to search for the right. We like to have a long-standing relationship with someone who may be potentially defending us in a courtroom.

For litigation in Florida we recommend www.NeJameLaw.com

Install an Alarm on Every Property You Purchase

Security is often overlooked by real estate investors who are more interested in paint colors, tile options and kitchen cabinet replacement. Our investor friend Lori taught us a valuable lesson about security. Unfortunately it was an expensive lesson that cost her thousands of dollars.

During Lori's early investment years, she purchased a two-story single-family home in a nice residential area which she planned to keep as a rental property. Lori went through all the usual renovation necessities including interior paint, flooring and replacement of kitchen cabinets and appliances. Lori and her husband John spent two months renovating this house and were relieved to finally finish. One day John decided to check on their empty house - (it was empty while they searched for a tenant). As John went to unlock the front door, he noticed that it had been pried open. On opening the front door, he was horrified to see what had happened inside.

All the newly painted walls were spoiled by graffiti, paint been poured onto the new hardwood floors, the kitchen appliances and ceiling fans had been stolen, the kitchen cabinets were destroyed, and even the drawer handles had been stolen. Lori and John were devastated as months of hard work and thousands of dollars had been wiped out. They had not considered installing an alarm system in their vacant property since the house was located in such a nice quiet neighborhood. This decision proved costly and even though they had homeowners insurance, it set them back several months, not to mention the additional out-of-pocket expenses that occurred while waiting for the insurance claim to be settled.

Since then Lori has purchased a wireless alarm system that they install in every vacant property. Once she had told us her horror story, we immediately went out and purchased our own wireless alarm system. You cannot be too careful when it comes to protecting your investment, so make sure your vacant properties are adequately protected so you do not suffer the same fate as Lori and John.

Always Have at Least 6 to 12 Months of Operating Costs

In real estate not only do we manage people, property, and investors, but we also have to manage our debt and credit.

Cash may be king but credit and debt help you buy the kingdom. By managing your debts correctly and making sure you have a financial cushion, you will be prepared if disaster strikes. Whether it is unexpected renovations, vandalism, natural disasters, or just plain bad luck, you may be faced with trials and tribulations that you *must* be prepared for.

Murphy's Law states 'What can go wrong, will go wrong." This law shouldn't paralyze you from taking risks due to the fear of something going wrong. Murphy's Law reminds you to *proceed with caution*.

You cannot account for every bad situation that may occur, but you can make sure your finances and debts are well managed. This way, when situations do pop up from time to time, you will be prepared.

After completing our very first project in 2003, we created a 'disaster fund' in which we set aside money from each completed project. These funds were not to be used for purchasing properties, renovation expenses, travel, disbursements, etc. The funds were to be saved strictly for use in emergency situations. In 2004, several hurricanes pounded the State of Florida forcing us to draw from our newly created disaster fund. These hurricanes were truly devastating and some of the rental properties we owned were damaged, forcing many tenants to move out.

Fortunately, only one of our investment houses was severely damaged while the others suffered minor damages. The hurricanes brought the real estate industry to a screeching halt. Comparably speaking, hurricanes are to Florida what earthquakes are to California.

When hurricanes hit, housing prices drop, repairmen become hot commodities and building materials become scare. Thankfully we were prepared for such a disaster by holding a reserve of 12 months of operating capital.

The insurance companies were dealing with tens of thousands of claims so the process of receiving a payout was severely delayed. Fortunately, we had saved funds and our repairs were completed in four weeks. If we had not saved funds towards operating costs, we would have been forced to wait four to six months to complete these repairs.

Some people would choose to use credit cards to float them through difficult times. Though credit cards can be a great source of help during emergencies, we prefer cash because it gives us a clear picture of where we stand with our finances.

If we had not been prepared, our business might have suffered the same fate as many other investors' businesses. We may have run out of money before we could get our business up and running again. Some of our investor colleagues did not adequately prepare and suffered massive losses due to lack of repair capital and lack of money to make loan payments when their rental income dried up. You must learn from their mistakes and always have enough money to carry your expenses for at least 12 months. By refraining from withdrawing some of your income and profits out of your business, you are setting up a personal insurance policy.

If you find you do not have enough cushioning, save diligently by using other incomes to pad your business account. Maybe it's time to cancel the cable TV or stop eating out so much? There are many ways to trim your expenses in order to save. You just have to be honest about where your money goes each month. Time after time we meet investors who make the crucial mistake of being under-funded; it is quite shocking to think how much they are risking. If you want to become a full time real estate investor but do not have a 12-month cushion, you are not ready to make that jump yet. Having 12 months of operating expenses will create stability and peace of mind.

Life Insurance Policies for You and Your Partner

Our company has bought and sold countless properties. At any given time our debt obligations owed and guaranteed by us could be as low as $200,000 or as high as several million. Amassing a large debt comes as a part of the real estate business investors must become comfortable with as it is part of the territory. Debt was the metaphoric 200 lb backpack that came along with our success. Being in a partnership, we did not want this debt burden to weigh us down financially if something were to happen to either of us.

As individuals we have very different life styles. One of us often flies back and forth between the US and Europe for family and international real estate deals, while the other travels more locally driving between 20,000 and 30,000 miles a year.

We realized that this amount of travel increased our exposure to potential accidents so should anything happen, neither one of us would want to be in business with the other partner's wife or family members. If something were to happen to one of us, that person's business interests would become part of his estate. The debts would still need to be paid and in order to do this, the business assets might need to be liquidated within the estate which could be time consuming and troublesome. For instance, if Matt were to die, his wife would become a 50% owner of his share in the company. Decisions could be at a deadlock if she and the other owners did not agree. To avoid this potential problem, we both carry life insurance policies which cover all the worst-case scenarios. The funds from these policies could be used in multiple ways such as to pay off the debts, loans or to buy out the new partners.

These policies are generally inexpensive and can range from $10,000 to several million dollars in coverage. Once you have acquired any substantial assets or debts, we recommend you speak with an insurance agent or financial advisor about your insurance options.

Beware of Seminars and Infomercials

You know those television infomercials touting 'get rich quick' methods of real estate investing? Some of these infomercials sell gateway courses designed to sell you other seminars and training products that claim to show you all the different ways you can find great real estate deals.

While some of these training tactics and seminars may be beneficial, we find that most of them sell unachievable pipe dreams promising uncountable riches and early retirement. The people running the seminars pitch ridiculous financial returns using techniques that are outdated and do not work anymore. Thanks to the Internet, all the information you need to find to become a successful investor is available at your fingertips.

One downside of all this readily available information is that more people have greater knowledge of market values resulting in smaller profit margins.

We are not here to bash or condemn seminars and infomercials but we want you to be aware that the same information being sold at these expensive seminars is mostly available for FREE on the Internet. You just have to take the time to look for it.

Most investors want to know where they can find good real estate deals. Try these places to start with:

For Sale by Owner real estate (FSBO)

We have found several deals in the FSBO market. These sellers attempt to save real estate commissions by listing their own homes and are generally less knowledgeable about market conditions. While commissions may be saved, the marketing of their property generally suffers, resulting in longer than normal sales times. This delay can create a sense of desperation for the seller creating great opportunities for you.

Tax Deed Sales

Tax Deed sales are our favorite source of real estate deals. We discuss this topic in depth in our book: Tax Deed Real Estate Investing - How We made over $1,000,000 in Two Years. The book is available at **tax-deed.com and Amazon.com** and is frequently listed on the top 10 real estate books in Amazon.

Foreclosures sold by banks REO (Real Estate Owned) offices

REO properties are foreclosed real estate that banks offer for sale. This means the original owner has vacated and the property is ready to be sold immediately! These REO departments can be found online or by contacting a local bank branch and asking for the relevant contact information.

Probate or estate sales

Specialized attorneys and real estate agents administer these types of sales. A probate sale involves the liquidation of property due to death. These sales are easily searchable via the Internet and are a great resource for real estate deals.

Local real estate attorneys

This source requires relationship building as most attorneys save their best deals for the people that they know. Try to network with as many attorneys as possible and nurture those relationships. Inform them that you are a real estate investor and ask if they would be willing to contact you should anything become available. Most real estate attorneys are used to being asked this so do not be afraid to approach them with request.

Vacant rental homes

Houses that have rental signs in the yard offer a great opportunity, especially if the house has been vacant for some time. If you notice a house that fits this description, contact the landlord and ask if he would consider selling the property. Vacant rental properties can be a thorn in a landlord's side as the houses turn from cash cows into cash bleeding liabilities. If the landlord will not consider selling, ask about a lease option deal. These deals involve putting down a large cash payment and renting the house. The idea behind this method is you try to find a tenant who will rent the property from you for more than the amount you are paying the landlord.

We are not big fans of the lease option method; it is one that is touted by some *low money / no money down* seminars and infomercials. We mention the technique because it is one you should be aware of. We do however know a few investors who make a good living solely focusing on acquiring empty rental properties on lease option deals.

You can also find rental properties on websites such as rentals.com and Craigslist. These website often list leads to lease option deals and desperate sellers.

These are just a few ideas without going into too much detail as a whole book could be written on all of these methods. Some creative thinking can result in limitless real estate deals. We would encourage you to choose one or two of our suggested methods and focus on those rather than trying them all.

Know when it's Time to Exit

When you become involved in the real estate business you will hear the saying, "Don't get emotionally attached to a property."

Many beginner investors cannot separate the idea of looking at an investment property subjectively and sometimes become emotionally attached. Word to the wise - Real estate is an investment to make money. Do not ever let your emotions control a deal.

Buying investment real estate is very different from buying a home you want to live in, even though your brain may tell you otherwise. When we began buying our first properties, we found it difficult to emotionally detach ourselves because we had invested so much time and effort into each project. There were instances where we rented renovated condos rather than selling them. We had spent months making them perfect and could not bear to part with them. We also wanted to see the smiles on potential tenants' faces as they saw these beautiful living spaces for the first time.

Our emotions altered our motivation for buying and it hindered us from selling the properties immediately. It was a flaw that we remedied quickly but our story is all too common.

You cannot make decisions based on emotions and you must look at each real estate deal as simply that - a deal. Each deal is simply a business transaction, which at the end of the day, is designed to financially beneficial while also providing someone with a beautiful place to live. Sometimes you may find it necessary to sell a property much sooner than you had planned which is fine because you should never become emotionally attached to real estate. Your plan is simple. Acquire, renovate, market, and then sell for a profit.

In 2007 when the real estate market began to downturn we were involved in a condo renovation project. Our financial investment was considerable and we were several months from completion. Once we saw the market begin to shift we had to make the difficult decision to sell prior to completion. This was a gut wrenching decision but it was either sell or take a heavy financial loss. By selling these condos to other investors for below market price, we were able to hedge some of our risk and potentially save tens of thousands of dollars.

Sometimes you will be faced with difficult decisions; it's part of the business. Do not be stubborn and pay special attention to what is happening in your local real estate market. Always have an exit strategy should the worst case scenario appear.

If you follow this simple rule and keep your emotions out of your decision making process, you will be well on your way to becoming a successful real estate investor.

CONTRACTS

The $43,000 Mistake - Almost

It is imperative that when you are purchasing a property, your contract states 'All days are calculated in business days.'

We love this rule and now use it with every contract. Without this rule, we would have lost a small fortune.

A few years ago we agreed to buy three parcels of land for $430,000, which we placed under contract and deposited 10% of the sales price in escrow ($43,000). Our contract stated that we were to close on the property within 90 days. We encountered some serious problems obtaining financing because the banks were less than enthusiastic lending to us because our experience in land development was minimal. Eventually, we found a bank willing to finance our project. However, we learned it would take five weeks to complete a commercial appraisal! The 90-day closing deadline appeared impossible to meet, thus meaning we would lose our $43,000 deposit.

As time passed and the closing deadline approached, the seller of the land was flooded with calls leading to offers higher than our full contract price. The seller was praying we would miss his closing deadline and default on our contract, allowing him to keep our deposit and sell his land for a higher price. As you can imagine, we were very upset and reluctant to lose our deposit. Can you imagine losing $43,000 due to a slow real estate appraisal?

Neither could we and we were determined not to let this happen.

The seller began hounding us to make sure we had completed all the tasks and due diligence needed to close on time. We fielded daily calls from his real estate agent and our agent - the phone rang constantly. The stress was overwhelming and it was taking a toll on our business relationship. Had we made a huge mistake? Were we in over our heads? Were we going to forfeit $43,000 we couldn't afford? Not if we could help it!

Realizing we had quite an emergency on our hands, we began to scour the contract looking for loopholes that would provide us with some sort of extension. After hours of reading, we finally found the loophole we so desperately needed. The seller and his agent told us that we needed to close on the property 90 days after the execution date of our contract. As we dove deeper into the contract, we saw the line that read, 'All days will be computed in business days.' The beauty of this phrase was that business days do not include federal holidays or weekends, so this gave us an extra 25 days to close and saved us from losing our $43,000 deposit.

This contract text was truly a blessing and saved our business deal and too this day, we always make sure we include it in all of our contracts.

Granted, the seller was not happy when we informed him that our actual closing date would be extended 25 days past his intended closing date. We did not care about the seller's irate reaction to the news, as we were so happy not to be losing the deal.

One way of avoiding this problem is to include a specific closing date in your sales contract (such as December 15th 2018). That being said, we suggest you try to avoid writing in an actual date when you are the purchaser. The reason for this is if you need extra time to close on a deal, writing an actual date may prevent you from extending or finding additional loopholes should issues occur.

Use the words 'business days' to apply to closing dates, inspection periods, finance periods, feasibility periods, or any date range. We encourage you to use this language to your advantage. The semantics of the contract can really make or break your deal.

There is a reason why important details are included in contracts in fine print, which make it even more important for you to over those details.

You never know when it just might save you $43,000.

Visit our forms sections at www.101rules.com for our recommended forms.

These 7 Words Can Save You Thousands

'All days are calculated in calendar days.'

This is inherently opposite to the previous rule on buying. When you are the seller, you want to put the pressure on the buyer to close as quickly as possible.

By adding an addendum stating 'All days are calculated in calendar days', it forces buyers to complete all their financing, inspections, due diligence, and closing in the quickest possible time.

If you write in the contract, 'Buyers have 10 calendar days to apply for financing', this language would count weekends and holidays as part of the 10 days.

Understand we do not include this language to alienate a potential buyer; however we do need to make sure that the contract does not allow buyers to delay closing.

Personally, we have never written a contract with the intention of taking anyone's deposit. There have been numerous times that we have allowed extensions even though we were well within our legal rights to take the buyer's deposit and to cancel the contract. Causing someone to lose their deposit is not the way to create good business relationships and you should avoid doing this whenever possible.

In addition to using 'calendar days', you can also write specific completion dates for the buyer's:

Due Diligence
Zoning
Inspection
Applications
Financing
Title Searches
Closing

Start Date = Sign Date

20 days to complete construction and repairs. Seems like a pretty simple sentence right? You would be surprised to find out that there can be *many* interpretations of how long this "20 day task" should actually take.

20 days from when the permit is pulled?

20 days, as in working days?

20 calendar days?

20 days including holidays?

20 days INCLUDING today?

As you can see there are many interpretations. The purpose of this rule is to help *define* specific dates and to make sure you maximize the productivity of the people you have working for you. This rule is not designed to be misleading or take unfair advantage but rather to make sure everyone is on the same page to avoid potential problems.

When we hire subcontractors, we make sure our contract language is very specific and that we expect them to begin work as soon as possible. If we sign a contract on the 3rd and it specifies 20 days for completion, by the end of the day of the 23rd day we expect the job to be finished.

If there is a holiday during this time period, the contractor should have taken that into consideration.

When dealing with contractors, it is possible you will hear an excuse such as, "Well you forgot that last Monday was a holiday so our workers had a 3 day weekend and that's why we are behind schedule." This type of excuse should never be tolerated. If the contractor agreed to complete the project in 20 days, the holidays should not be an excuse for failing to complete on time.

If a contractor had to pull a permit and that took four days, this should be considered part of the 20-day completion deadline unless your contract specifies otherwise.

Do not get suckered into these types of *delays* as they will be costly. Contractors are supposed to be professionals and are expected to consider all reasonable factors. Make sure you hold all contractors accountable for completion dates. Many times we include a penalty for every day that the job is not completed. This really makes a big difference. Obviously there are times when unforeseeable circumstances happen, so use common sense and good judgment. If you find a contractor is falling further and further behind, this is a sign of the way things will continue.

This rule concerning *start dates* will clarify exactly when job projects should be completed by and help reduce disagreements.

Define Penalties and Hold Backs with Your Contractor

Time is money, literally! So when money is on the line, penalties are the only way to enforce a contractor or sub contactor to complete their work on time.

Without monetary penalties in place, some contractors see contracts as a 'written handshake' which may not be enforced. We like to have contracts backed up by penalties to keep contractors in line. Penalties should be set at a dollar amount per day. On one occasion, our contractor failed to meet his completion deadline on six condo units and was therefore bound by a $150 penalty per day per condo unit.

In addition to accrued penalties, you can also increase the amount you hold back for the punch list (this is the list of final miscellaneous tasks prior to job completion). Most contractors prefer a hold back amount of 10%. For example, if there is a painting job that is costing $1000 and you pay $300 upfront for supplies then another $600 when the job is completed, you would hold back a further $100. Unfortunately this $100 is not very much. Sometimes you will find that a contractor will walk out on the remaining amount because the labor costs involved exceeds the hold back amount so be aware of this.

We suggest the following addition to your work contract: In the eventuality that the 'due date' is passed, make sure that your contract states that the 'hold back' amount would be increased to 20% or 30% so you can collect late penalties.

This way, if the contractor accrues penalties, you have a dollar amount remaining which you can deduct the penalties from. We have found ourselves in situations where the penalties exceeded our hold back and we were unsuccessful in retrieving those penalties.

Remember that each delay costs you money out of your pocket and can only be recouped if your contract has the correct penalty and hold back provisions!

All Contracts Should be Assignable When You are the Buyer

An assignable contract means you are able to sell the property by assigning the contract to another buyer before you close. Why make a contract assignable if you intend on proceeding forward with an agreement to buy?

There are times when you are under contract to buy a piece of real estate and other investors or business acquaintances become interested in your property. Sometimes it is more convenient to take a small profit on the transaction by assigning the contract to someone else and moving on to the next deal.

When assigning contracts, the only real risk is whether the assignee will follow through and complete the transaction. We recommend you only enter into an assignment deal with people you know will follow through.

In some instances a contract will still enforce your liability as the buyer even though it is assignable. In other words, if you or the person you assign it to does not close on the property, you will still be liable under the obligations you signed and agreed to. You must beware of such situations and make sure you have an attorney read the contract. Most contracts we have dealt with have already included an assignment clause so it can be as simple as checking a box to allow for assignments. If the seller is hesitant to deal with you because of the potential of assignment, try explaining that assignments do not release you from any obligation to close.

Some real estate investors make fortunes by assigning contracts to other people without ever actually owning the properties. Other investors are even willing to pay a premium for assigned contracts on great properties. Do not miss out on this potential for easy profit! Make sure all your buying contracts have the ability to be assigned… it might be the easiest profit you will ever make on a property you never have to buy!

Contract Penalties Can be Your Best Friend

This rule is a great deterrent and a potential moneymaker or money saver, depending on the situation. There have been many times when we have made extra profits by extending our closing date.

Most of the time people have legitimate reasons for extending a closing date. Even though these reasons may be well founded, as a seller, you should be compensated for the delays. If you are not compensated, it will likely cost *you* money. If you hold mortgages or hard money loans on investment properties you are selling, closing delays cost you interest on a daily basis. Why not recoup these costs?

We set our contract penalty in the $75 to $150 a day range depending on the cost of the property and find this amount to be reasonable. When implementing penalties, always be upfront in your explanation to the buyers so they understand that a speedy closing is essential. Sometimes extending the closing date is necessary; just try to make sure you are compensated.

Rule of thumb: If you make the penalty too high, chances are the buyer will not sign the contract. Make sure the amount of your penalty is fair and reasonable.

It is in your best interest to sell your property as quickly as possible so you do not want to kill a deal by being greedy. Penalty contract language is designed to be more of a deterrent because, if left to their own devices, buyers' can be slow to close and these delays incur extra holding costs for you. Chances are you never have to enforce the penalty but it is in there should you need it.

It is definitely an extra perk to be able to make an extra few hundred dollars at the closing table due to a buyer's tardiness.

One final point: make sure your contract states 'every calendar day' not 'every business day'. Failure to include the correct word could give the buyer extra grace periods on weekends and federal holidays.

All Construction and Repair Contracts Must Have a Final 'Dead Date'

Dead dates are dates for final completion in which you are able to exit a contractor's agreement if the completion dates are not met. Final dead dates are important because even though you may have a contract that includes delayed work penalties, you cannot let those delays continue indefinitely. In other words, there has to be an exit strategy should the contractors' delays continue.

On many occasions our General Contractor (or GC) has passed their work completion dates and therefore accrued penalties. In one instance, our GC took almost six months to complete a two-month project and because we did not have a dead date of completion, we were tied to the contract indefinitely. Even though the GC penalties continued to accrue, our project fell further and further behind.

If we had known then what we know now, our contract would have included a final dead date of 90 days after the project had started. Since the GC estimated his work would be finished in 60 days, this would have allowed us to exit the agreement 30 days later without further financial obligation to the contractor.

After we learned about final dead dates we looked back at prior projects and estimated that we could have saved ourselves tens of thousands of dollars. Remarkably, these deadlines will help you control the project and unburden yourself of some of the hostage-like feelings you will experience when a GC is not performing as promised.

This approach should be taken with every single contracting trade that you do business with including painting, concrete, framing, and so on. Each trade contractor should be accountable for finishing on time and within budget.

This rule works especially well when used with our penalties rule.

CONTRACTORS

Trust but Verify

People you meet in the real estate business will be quick to give you all of their success stories. These people include: contractors, contacts, appraisers, real estate agents, property managers, mortgage brokers, subcontractors, bankers, friends, relatives, and....well, you get the idea.

On rare occasions, investors share stories of their errors, mistakes, and mishaps along the way. People have a habit of embellishing the truth and can often mislead, candy-coat, and omit crucial information. Therefore, it is imperative to pay attention to these experiences prior to hiring workers or forming partnerships. As you interview potential people, trust what they say but *always* verify the information. Hence, results should be measured, inspected, and verified.

The Key: You should only trust someone with your project, investment, or business after you have verified that they are worthy of your trust. This can save you tens of thousands of dollars.

Several years ago we were finishing work on our first investment home and were anxious to place the property up for sale. During the last few days of the project we became overwhelmed and physically tired due to the countless labor hours we had put into the project. All we had left to complete was the exterior painting of the wood trim which seemed simple but turned out to be very labor intensive. To be quite honest, painting was not our favorite pastime.

During our first paint-prepping day, a man named José approached us looking for work. He explained he was down on his luck but was an experienced painter who would be willing to finish our trim painting for only $250. We were expecting the quote to be more in the $500 to $800 range due to the amount of work needing to be completed. Accordingly, this low bid amount should have been our first red flag. There was a large amount of trim to paint, most of which needed sanding and scraping. Since we were in no mood to paint, we ignored our red flag and hired José anyway.

The next day, José showed up on time but without paintbrushes, paint clothes, and ladders. He had absolutely nothing. We began to wonder if José's low bid was due to a misunderstanding of the work expectations. We should have fired him then and there but as we said before, we were anxious to complete the house so we decided to let José use our painting equipment and supplies.

Urgently, we needed to get this job completed now, as in yesterday! Later that evening after working, José called us to let us know he was finished. The next morning we went to the house to view José's work. It was a complete disaster!

José had to ask a friend to come help him because he was overwhelmed with the workload. They were both covered from head to toe in paint and we are not exaggerating when we tell you it looked as if a paint bomb had exploded right above their heads! José and his friend had wasted at least five gallons of paint and it was all over the driveway, the lawn and the walls they weren't supposed to touch. They even broke our ladder!

After we deducted the cost of the ladder, José and his friend pocketed a grand sum of $150 and we would have gladly paid double that just to get rid of them. In addition, we spent eight hours the next day touching up their fantastic paint job… so much for saving time.

After this disaster, we attempt to obtain references and then always check them diligently. Notably, you must always verify that whoever you hire can do what they say they can do, even if it is the simplest of jobs.

It is impossible to count the number times we received suspect "references" from subcontractors. After verification, many times it turned out the subcontractor had completed their work inadequately, receiving numerous complaints, or even worse, walking off the job without notice!

Remember, many subcontractors are bold enough to apply for jobs in fields they are unqualified to work in due to the fact that most employers never check their references. Do not be one of these falsified reference believers...verify, verify and verify again!

If you have a subcontractor who tells you he has just completed electrical work in an 80-unit apartment complex, ask for his General Contractor's contact details and verify the quality of workmanship; better yet, visit the work site and ask to see it. You never know, the subcontractor may have started on a project that he was fired from due to lack of experience or incompetence...it happens all the time.

Trust what people say but always verify; it will save you time, headaches and a lot of money.

Go to a Contractor's Office and See Where They Work

Some contractors work out of their home, which is fine but generally if working on a larger construction project, we prefer to hire larger scale contractors who operate out of an office space.

If you deal with a small contractor you may find that a 12-condo renovation project is too much for him to handle so finding the correct company for the appropriate job size is essential.

The contractor interview process should go beyond having them visit your job site. You must meet with these contractors at their office so you can see what type of operation they run. This will provide great insights into their work and who they associate with.

We recently interviewed a few contractors for a medium sized condo renovation project. After we chose the contractor, we received the necessary permits and work began. It only took a week for us to know we had hired the wrong contractor so we decided to set up a meeting in his office. If we had taken this office meeting *before* we hired him, he would have immediately been eliminated from the prospect list.

While sitting in the office waiting for the meeting to begin, we overheard some conversations and phone calls. The number of complaints we heard in this short period of time was astounding. The receptionist was running interference for the contractors, laborers were complaining about not being paid and two employees argued behind closed doors about projects being too far behind schedule. Despite us checking the contractor's references, the real issues weren't apparent until we went behind the scenes!

It had only taken 10 minutes of being in the office to realize this company was a disaster. We negotiated a deal with them to try to finish the project but in the end we terminated our work agreement due to missed deadlines. A pre-hiring office meeting would have eliminated this situation entirely.

Request and Check References from all Contractors

Checking references was one of the hardest things we had to force ourselves to do. It is so easy to collect the reference contacts and not follow through. We do not know of any real estate investors who enjoy checking references but it is just part of the business so you had better get used it.

Make sure you contact every reference you are given! You will be amazed at the information that is given to you. Sometimes the references may not be 100% satisfied with the contractor and will provide you with valuable insights into the problems they experienced.

Remember that no contractor is perfect but each should have a solid history of happy customers who would be pleased to rehire them due to the quality of work. We attempt to obtain references from people who are either currently working with, or have just finished working with the contractor. Some of the contractors' past clients often turn a blind eye to the job issues and are relieved when the project is over so ask if you can visit the work site so you can see the end result for yourself.

This rule not only applies for contractors but also for tenants. ALWAYS check the tenant references. Again, you will be surprised what information people will give you regarding the person you are researching. People love to talk, and they especially love talking about others.

In one example, we were driving around a neighborhood where one of our rental houses was located, searching for someone to repair a damaged pool pump.

We noticed a pool company truck parked outside a house and a man walking towards it. We stopped and asked the man if he could do some pool cleaning and repair work for us the following day, to which he agreed. We noticed another man coming out of the house the repairman had just left, and decided to ask him for a reference. It was a good job we asked because this homeowner was very unhappy with his pool service!

The pool repairman had made numerous visits to fix a 'faulty' pool pump that he finally determined as un-repairable. The repairman was then hired to install a new pump but there were problems with the installation. We offered to look at the pump for the homeowner and after inspection, we found that the new pump was not new at all; it was used! To make things worse, the used pump had bad ball bearings in it and was making a horrible grinding noise. What a valuable reference that turned out to be and needless to say we did not hire the pool repairman!

Unfortunately we find that many 'craftsmen' do shoddy work or are less than qualified. Asking for two or three references from recently completed jobs helps you eliminate most of these unsavory repairmen.

Just simply ASKING for references can provide a sense of what type of work they do. We recently remodeled a house that needed 1200+ square feet of tile installation. Our main tile contractor was on vacation so we made some calls to set up bids and interviews. We asked each contractor to bring us photos from past projects. Three contractors visited us at different times throughout the day and after explaining the job details, we asked for references and the photos.

One contractor came prepared with both the photos and a list of references. Another came with pictures but no references but proceeded to hunt through his phone for names and numbers of recent jobs. The third had pictures but seemed reluctant to provide us with references.

Even the simple process of asking for references and pictures helps you weed out the unqualified suspects. Photos can be deceiving so you must check the references. Stacks of names and phone numbers are useless if you do not verify them.

Set a Schedule and Daily Penalties if Contractors Fall Behind

It doesn't matter whether you hire a General Contractor, subcontractor, painter, tile installer, whoever... just ensure that you have a final 'dead date' of completion (see rule on dead dates). Penalties should be included in the contract and enforced if the work is not completed by the due dates. Too often the people we hire fall behind schedule and that happens for many reasons. Some reasons are valid, while most are not. These people are motivated by one thing only, money. Reducing a worker's money daily is usually MORE than enough incentive to 'encourage' him to finish by the dead-line date.

Once we hired a contractor to renovate 4 condos. Unfortunately we picked the wrong contractor. The job should have taken 45-60 days but instead, ended up taking 180 days. This delay cost us over $15,000 in additional interest and holding costs so we forced the contractor to reduce his bill by $12,000. These penalties saved us on a short-term basis but in the end we should have fired the contractor. Ultimately the situation was far more costly because during the delays, the real estate market down-turned causing us to lose our pre-qualified buyers. We were then forced to hold and rent the condos due to the lack of buyers. If we had not let those delays occur, we would have sold the condos immediately after completion.

Luckily, we learned from this mistake and the additional two condos that needed renovating were awarded to a different General Contractor who agreed to complete them in 60 days. The penalties for failing to complete on time were doubled and a dead date was added. In the end, we ended up saving about $6,000 on a $50,000 contract.

While paying attention to saving costs on the bid amount, you must pay special attention to costs that impact you as an investor in the form of stress, time, money, and lost opportunity. You should always be compensated if a contractor cannot complete their tasks by a set date.

Keep Close Supervision of the Subcontractors on Projects but Do Not Micromanage

At some point you have to learn to trust the people you hire. During our early renovation projects, we completed almost all the work ourselves. Those days were long and grueling but necessary to keep costs low.

We certainly hired our fair share of inadequate subcontractors that created plenty of headaches for us. We tried to micromanage these contractors thinking this would reduce the issues. What was the result? Our productivity levels took a nose dive and instead of being out in the field searching for our next big deal, we were stuck at the project site trying to micromanage the workers!

Eventually we learned to identify the problematic subcontractors and relieve them of their duties. Despite knowing better in regards to micromanaging, we assembled a new team and continued to watch them like hawks. For example, we purchased a nice two-bedroom, one-bathroom condo right next to Universal Studios in Orlando for a steal of a price! The condo was in *very* good condition but some tile updating was needed in the kitchen and bath areas. We called our tile contractor Rick and put him to work. Even though it was a small project, it required plenty of tedious detail work such as mosaics. We added these touches in order to really showcase the condo and make it sell quickly!

During day three on the job we took Rick out to lunch and were involved in a conversation that went like this….

Rick: "Do you like the work I did on your other projects?"

Us: "Yes, of course."

Rick: "Have I done something wrong on this job or previous jobs?"

Us: "Not at all, why?"

Rick: "Because you guys won't leave me alone to do my job. Since you know I do a good job, you can trust me to work alone. It's distracting to have you guys at the jobsite all the time watching over me. I feel like you don't trust me."

Our conversation with Rick was very enlightening. We had dealt with so many inadequate subcontractors that we had become paranoid and now we were ruining our relationship with Rick whose work quality never disappointed us!

We immediately realized our mistakes and apologized for intruding on Rick's workspace. We were at the jobsite too often, asking too many questions and slowing him down.

When you begin in real estate you think of each deal like a child you want to nurture and protect. This is understandable but remember you cannot do everything yourself all the time. You have to learn to trust others to complete tasks you may not be able to complete yourself. Once you learn to do this, your productivity levels will sky rocket.

Understand where your skills are best put to use and let others handle the rest without micromanaging them. We learned our time was better spent researching new deals and marketing our properties rather than breathing down our subcontractor's neck.

Give Praise to Your Workers When Work Quality is High

When working on a project that requires the hiring of subcontractors', ask yourself the following questions:

How can I create long lasting relationships with them so they will want to complete future work for me?

How can I encourage them to complete work at their highest standards?

How can I motivate them to finish on time?

How can I motivate them to finish under budget?

Take the time to get to know your workers and find out what they value. Believe it or not we have had workers explain that they left other jobs because they were not allowed enough time to take a lunch break. If their previous employers had taken a few minutes to find out their grievances, this situation could have been avoided.

Maybe there was an occasion when a worker needed to pick up a spouse or child from work or school. In this case, *time* was their need. In return for your flexibility, the workers may be open to other requests from you such as working additional hours to compensate for missed time.

On one occasion we purchased land that was so badly overgrown with brush and vegetation that the weeds had grown as high as small trees! We even received a notice from the City warning us of possible fines of up to $500 per day for not maintaining the land.

We decided to hire Cliff to maintain the land. Cliff was an older retired man who lived nearby our land and owned a large tractor that was perfect for mowing and maintaining our property. Whenever we were in the vicinity of Cliff's house, we would visit and thank for him for the great work he was doing for us.

We really enjoyed chatting with Cliff and he loved to tell us about the different projects he was working on. Cliff certainly liked to stay busy during his retirement.

After the fourth month, we were so happy with Cliff's meticulous maintenance of our land that we gave him a gift card to use at his favorite home improvement store.

Cliff was dumbfounded by our gift card gesture as considered his job payment to be enough. We like to build relationships by going and above and beyond peoples' expectations, no matter how small the job may be. Cliff excitedly treated himself to some new power tools that he needed to complete repairs on his own home.

We eventually sold our land but we still hire Cliff for any lawn maintenance jobs we have in the Daytona area. Most importantly, our friendship with Cliff continues to this day.

In another example, we faced a disgruntled painting crew who were being poorly compensated by the General Contractor we hired. We provided the workers with ice cold Coronas at the end of their shift. We did this for three days to thank them for their hard work. The workers morale improved and the job was completed on time with good attention to detail.

When the General Contractor could no longer find the jobs for these workers, we received calls from them to see if we had any available painting work.

Genuine praise and gratitude go a very long way so always remember to praise and take care of the people you hire and they will be loyal to you for years to come.

Be Sure to Verify all Contractor Receipts

Sometimes contractors can be very difficult to deal with and somewhat rough around the edges. This doesn't mean that you should let them take advantage of you as some of them will try to.

Our investor friend Jenny had just purchased her first rental home when in the midst of the renovation project; her contractor was forced to move away leaving her project at a standstill.

Desperate to avoid major delays, Jenny hired a family friend named Josh to complete her renovations. After only one week, problems with Josh occurred that Jenny did not know to how handle. Jenny was particularly concerned about firing Josh and being left without a contractor once again so she asked us to take over management of the renovation. We decided to help out under the condition that Jenny would give us full control over the project. We did not want to involve her with every decision as this would delay the project even further.

The first thing we did was to look over Josh's receipts to make sure all his purchases were justified. It appeared to us that Josh was buying more supplies then he could possibly need so we asked him to meet with us to discuss this concern. During the meeting we asked Josh about the extra supply purchases to which he had no explanation. Josh proceeded to become quite irritated and defensive and he kept asking why we cared since Jenny never bothered him about such matters. We explained that it was our job to manage the renovation and keep on budget to which Josh convinced us he was free of any wrong-doing. We decided to give Josh the benefit of the doubt.

At our next meeting with Josh, he handed us a receipt for 30 gallons of interior paint. The house was only 1500 square feet with three-bedrooms and two-bathrooms so it was impossible that he would need such a large amount of paint. Josh argued that he needed this paint for the job and once again became defensive and irate when we questioned this purchase. It is common practice for unscrupulous contractors to charge extra supplies to one client and then use the extra supplies on their next job while billing their next client once more. This is what we suspected Josh was doing to Jenny.

As time passed, Josh acted more aggressively and continued to give us unwarranted supply receipts. We decided enough was enough and it was time to fire Josh and find a new contractor to take over Jenny's renovation. We had been very patient with Josh but he was now taking advantage and it had to stop.

When it came to the uncomfortable firing conversation, Josh became enraged and at that point we knew the correct decision had been made. Know when it is time to stop being cool and start being assertive when dealing with contractors who you suspect are acting dishonestly.

Never be afraid to sit down with a contractor to discuss purchases. Remember this is your money and it is your job to keep your projects on budget. Ignoring this rule will cost you in many ways.

Make Sure Your Contractor Is Bonded and Insured

Being a real estate investor you will learn that contractors, subcontractors, tradesmen, and laborers have different levels of skills. We learned that General Contractors are only needed for larger scale projects and so we employ individual tradesmen, laborers, or subcontractors for smaller jobs. This allows us to stay on budget and have more control over the individual workers rather than just a single General Contractor.

Some of these companies along with their workers have insurance while others do not. Why would we need to make sure they have insurance? In cases where we hire an interior painter, dry-waller or carpet installer, we generally do not check their insurance coverage as those types of jobs have very little injury risk. Now remember this is *our* policy in regards to insurance for these types of workers and we're not advising you follow suit. You have to make your own decision about what is acceptable to you.

Other trades such as plumbing, electrical, roofing, exterior painting, foundation, and framing present a much higher risk of injury.

Plumbers use torches, metal cutters, and work in confined spaces. Electricians work with high amperages that can easily kill. Foundation work involves heavy-duty machinery where injury is common. Framers, exterior painters and roofers often use ladders and scaffolding with no safety harnesses so they are at risk of falling. These are jobs the types where it is essential we verify adequate insurance coverage prior to us hiring them.

If you hire a General Contractor with valid insurance, any accidents to his employees should be covered under his policy. If the General Contractor has no valid insurance and an employee was injured on your jobsite, that worker might seek financial damages from you. It is very possible this could be in the form of a lawsuit and regardless of whether or not you were at fault; it will cost you money to defend it. This is why you must also carry good insurance with high liability limits.

To avoid lawsuits, always verify that anyone you hire has necessary *valid* insurance. We recommend that you include the insurance requirements within any work agreements you sign. Be sure to specify that their insurance must be valid for the entire duration of the job. This prevents them for using temporary insurance. In our experience, the most common General Liability Insurance coverage starts at $1,000,000 and goes up from there. Some companies will carry much larger coverage amounts. This usually depends on the type of risk involved in the work being carried out and the number of people employed.

The insurance held by the contractor does not absolve you from providing a safe work area. As a property owner you still have the obligation to provide a safe, negligent-free work area.

What is a bond and why is it important?

A bond is a financial assurance (similar to an insurance policy) that a contractor will complete a job to satisfaction. Bonds cover such issues as a General Contractor defaulting on paying subcontractors and suppliers or a contractor walking off a job. For example, if a contractor installed an expensive front door in your home but failed to the supplier pay for the door, the bond would cover this cost rather than your door being repossessed by the supplier. A bond also covers such negligence as property damage and lost or stolen materials from the jobsite. Since bonds are kept valid by premium payments, always make sure to ask the contractor for proof of validity and ask for both the bond number and certification.

Always make sure your contractors are bonded and insured as just being bonded is not enough. Make sure the contractor supplies you with proof and don't just take their word for it.

Do Not Be Afraid To Fire Contractors, Subcontractors, or Any Hired Help

We cannot begin to count how many horror stories we have heard of people getting lumbered with subcontractors who simply do not perform up to par. It is very easy to be a conflict-avoider or to be swayed by a smooth talking subcontractor but beware if you fall victim to this, it will cost you large amounts of money.

We once purchased six apartments in a self-contained building. We decided to identically renovate all the apartments in order to save time and money and we assumed it would be easy to find a subcontractor to complete the work.

We interviewed 12 General Contractors and finally decided Terry was the man for the job. The reason we picked Terry over the other candidates was because he provided a professional portfolio book containing photos of the renovation projects he and his team had worked on. Terry was a bit of a fast talker but we found him to be very organized which is an essential trait to look for in a General Contractor.

Terry and his team began working on the renovation project which was scheduled to be completed within 55 days. The demolition went quickly but then work began to slow down. Terry and his team began to show up late and take four day weekends. Sometimes we would arrive at the job site at two o'clock in the afternoon and none of Terry's crew was anywhere to be found.

There always seemed to be a convenient excuse as to why the work project had slowed down and according to Terry, nothing was his fault. Eventually we grew tired and met with Terry to explain that if things did not change, we would be forced to find another General Contractor to take over the project. Switching General Contractors was problematic for us because Terry had applied for and remained in possession of all the construction permits.

If we fired Terry and hired a new General Contractor, we would have to apply for new permits. This would set us back several weeks resulting in expensive extra holding costs.

Another week passed and the work slowed even further so we were forced to make a drastic decision. We sat down with Terry and informed him we would be terminating his work contract immediately due to his failure to meet deadlines. He responded with his usual fast-talking but we had had enough and our minds were made up. Terry would not be receiving another chance. If we had fired Terry when the problems first arose, our project would have been completed six months earlier than it was completed. This mistake cost us tens of thousands of dollars.

It is normal for certain problems to arise during a project but pay attention to warning signs as they appear. If you see those signs more than twice, it is likely they will continue to show themselves so you must take action immediately. Listen to your gut and take the appropriate action, as it will pay off in the long run.

Never Hire Your Friends!

Friends, how many of us have them? Friends, people you can depend on in needy times, there is nothing better.

We had a friend named Bobby who was eager to help out whenever we needed him. Bobby called us one day and asked if we had anything he could do as he had lost his job and needed some work while he searched for new employment. We liked Bobby and embraced the opportunity to help someone we trusted.

At the time of Bobby's request for work, we had a house that needed painting and were in the midst of searching for a new painting contractor. It was a busy time and most painting contractors were booking jobs weeks and months in advance and the ones who were available were charging unreasonable prices. We decided to offer Bobby the job since he told us he had some painting experience. He was quite happy to accept and we were able to negotiate a rate that was fair to both parties involved. We instructed Bobby to pick out neutral colors for the house and gave him color swatch examples for him to pick from. All Bobby had to do was go to the hardware store and give the color swatches to the sales associate. Seems simple right?

After a few days, we decided to stop by the house to see how the painting was progressing. As we pulled up to the house we were shocked; the exterior paint was a ghastly bright yellow color! The worst part was the exterior paint job was almost finished. We asked Bobby why he had chosen such a horrible paint color. He explained he thought the color was nice and that the neutral colors we had chosen were particularly bland and unoriginal. We then proceeded to go inside the house. The interior walls were light purple with black accents; it was the worst paint job we had ever seen. Bobby was extremely offended that we did not like his choice of paint colors and we had no option but to terminate our agreement. Unfortunately our friendship was never the same after this and we learnt the very important rule about not hiring your friends.

Be Particular Because You Are Paying The Bills!

When we began investing in real estate, one of the first important rules our mentors instilled in us was to surround ourselves with a great professional team. This would include attorneys, accountants and real estate agents. It took a while to find the right people and as we met new professionals, we found personalities differed greatly. Our personalities are more laid back and less aggressive so it was important for us to work with people who we were compatible with.

We once worked with an attorney named Charles who was referred to us by a family friend. During our second meeting with Charles we began to feel particularly uncomfortable. He always seemed to be rushing us and we could not help feeling as if he was not giving us the attention we required. Charles also made us feel like he was doing *us* a favor by working with us. This has been something we have experienced with several attorneys. Sometimes they seem to have this 'better than' attitude and eventually we became tired of feeling as if we were working for them.

One day we met an attorney named Bruce. Bruce always answered our telephone calls personally, was very accommodating with appointment times and did not bill us for every second of his time. His personality was laid back like ours and he always made time for us, particularly when we needed him the most. During a meeting, we told Bruce about our past attorney experiences and in particular how some of them made us feel as if it was a privilege for us to be working with them. Bruce explained that this was a common complaint he received from new clients who had left their previous attorneys.

Bruce's opinion was that attorneys work for their clients and that the clients pay the attorneys salary, not the other way around. He also explained that this should be the way of thinking towards any professional person we hire including accountants, real estate agents and contractors. His final point was that if any professional people made us feel uncomfortable in any way, they were not people we should be hiring.

We are sure you have felt the same way sitting in an attorney's office. Always remember that you are the one paying the bills and that you should expect a certain level of service and respect from everyone you do business with. Do not ever accept anything less!

ACCOUNTING

Don't Find a Good Accountant, Find a GREAT Accountant

What good are your newly found record keeping skills if you do not have a professional accountant to decipher them?

NO GOOD AT ALL!

When we first formed our company, we were introduced to an accountant with whom we became comfortable. After two years of buying and selling properties and using his services, we realized he was a good accountant but not a great one.

We then interviewed three different accountants that were referred to us by other real estate investors and attorneys. After the interviews it became painfully obvious that our accountant was not as competent in our area of business as we had thought. We decided to hire someone who was more specialized in real estate accounting and who was very proactive about making sure we had the maximum tax deductions from:

Mileage	Work clothing
Communications	Utilities
Cell phones	Storage
Home offices	Meal expenses
Laptops	Entertainment

The above list was quite extensive and our new accountant explained how many of these deductions our old accountant had missed. These deductions could have saved us thousands of dollars on our taxes!

Our new accountant gave us detailed instructions on how to keep track of and document the deductible items. This documentation of 'write offs' helped reduce our tax liability at the end of the year and saved us a small fortune.

It only takes a few minutes a day to keep this information up to date and while it was something we did not like doing at first, now we have learned to enjoy and appreciate the security of keeping good tax records.

Keep an Interest-Bearing Bank Account for Larger Dollar Transactions

It pays to be thrifty… literally. Over the course of time we have invested conservatively and have been able to amass not only real estate, but also some cold hard cash.

At first when we had some money in the bank we did not think too much about it. To us cash was just a tool we used to acquire, fix and flip properties. But after a while we realized each time we had money sitting in our bank account, we were being robbed. The bank was using our money to make a profit without paying us a penny.

After doing some bank research, we found some banks that were offering interest-bearing business accounts. These interest rates weren't in the 0.01% range either; they were higher rates that made a real difference to our business.

Whether it is $5,000, $50,000, or $200,000, move that money into an interest-bearing account and make that money work for you. Do not let the banks use your money without paying you for it. It sounds so simple but we meet so many people who do not utilize this income method. Put your capital to work.

For example if you have $50,000, a year's interest at 4.0% interest rate you will make $166.66 in the first month. After compounding month after month that would be an extra $2,037.08 added to your bottom line! Think about that…an additional $2037.08 for moving your money to the correct business account! Do not be afraid to switch banks either. The more cash you accumulate over your investing career, the more significant these numbers will become. You will feel great each time you look at your monthly statement knowing the bank did not use your money for free!

Pick Your Bank Wisely and Develop a Relationship

We have dealt with many banks over the years, big and small and our experiences have ranged from wonderful to absurd. We have grown to cherish the relationships we have with our current banking professionals while also severing relationships with banks who were not supportive.

In the beginning we did not pay much attention or thought to where we chose to bank. We figured all banks were about the same in regards to their fees and customer service.

Were we wrong!

Our relationship with our first bank was very one-sided. We had a relationship and they had a customer whom they viewed as just a number. We found this out one day after asking for a cashier's check, which our bank had been issuing us for free for many years.

We needed to obtain a check to pay for a property at an auction and approached the teller asking politely for one in the amount of $15,000. The teller said that we would need to fill out a request for $15,008. When asked why, the teller explained they were charging us $8 for the cashier's check because of their 'new policy'. We stated that we had never been charged before and that we would like the fee to be waived but the teller refused to do this.

When we asked to speak the branch manager, the teller looked us right in the eyes and said, "I'll get the manager but he will not waive the fee for you."

Sure enough the manager also said no! We had been banking with the company for over three years holding multiple accounts with healthy balances. Soon we grew tired of the lack of care the bank was showing us and said, "We would hope you will reconsider waiving this ridiculous fee. We are good customers so either waive the fee or we will withdraw all of our money right now." The teller looked at us angrily and said she would be right back.

The teller wasn't leaving to talk to the manager to remove the fees; she was leaving to bring us a cashier's check for the whole balance in the accounts and all over an $8 fee! We will not name the bank (it is one of the largest in 'America') but needless to say, we will not be opening another account with them. They have a blatant disregard for customer service and only care about profit.

We took our cashier's check to a much smaller friendlier bank, explained our situation, and a new relationship was formed. This bank was more than happy to issue us with checks at no charge, and still do to this day. Our new bank respects us and treats us as if we were their only customers.

Remember at the end of the day you are doing the bank a favor by depositing your money with them. They are not doing you the favor. Does a bank really *need* you? No, not really but a good bank should always treat you as a cherished customer.

Not all large banks are evil fee-sucking empires and some actually do care about their customers. Our experiences though have proven multiple times that the smaller community banks and credit unions are more personable and forgiving.

Banks are in the business to provide services *and* make money. We do not expect these services to be free and are happy to pay for them in certain circumstances. Your bank should show by its actions that you are a valued customer and that it cares about you as much as it does about making a profit. Do not ever be afraid to move banks; it's a freeing experience.

When choosing a bank, consider the following:

Are there minimum balance requirements to avoid fees?
Do they have free online bill pay?
Do they have online syncing to your accounting software such as QuickBooks?
Do they offer free checks?
Do they charge for cashier's checks or money orders?
Are there statement costs?
Do they charge for imaging checks?
Are they open on Saturdays? (often overlooked)
What are their requirements for business loans and personal loans?
Do they offer private loan funding?

What are their Merchant Account fees for accepting credit cards?
What do they charge for Payroll Services?
Do they offer interest bearing accounts?

As you can see a bank is much more than just a place to park your money, so choose wisely!

Profits Are Made When You Buy, Not When You Sell

This is definitely a top 10 rule and applies to every type of real estate. If you do not pay the correct amount for the property when you buy, you are destined for failure and financial loss. Don't believe us? Just ask the millions of people who overpaid for real estate before the last real estate downturn and who are now in foreclosure.

The lack of research and due diligence is the most common reason investors overpay for a property. When you properly research property value, holding costs, repair costs, and selling expenses, your chances for profit and success will greatly increase.

A friend of ours named John purchased a house for $62,000. It was a ranch style three-bed, two-bath home with no garage or pool. It was located in a sub-average neighborhood with home prices hovering around $80,000. John thought the house was a good deal but we thought otherwise. The bottom line was that John had not adequately completed his research.

First of all we knew that just selling the house with standard real estate commissions would cost $4800.

Once we had finished our calculations including repairs, loan interest, taxes, insurance, staging the property, utilities, and closing costs, we found that John's total expenses would exceed any potential profit. John eventually sold the house for $79,450. The buyers even talked him into helping with part of the closing costs, which made his losses worse! When all was said and done, John lost $2200 and six months of his life.

The moral here is profit is made when you buy, not when you sell so do your research! If you research correctly, you will be turning down deals but your profits will be far higher.

Do your research, be thorough, and be profitable! Visit the www.101rules. com/tools to see our profit spreadsheet!

Keep Detailed Spreadsheets and Accounting Records

Our company uses Excel spreadsheets to enter every transaction we complete - all receipts, costs and incomes are recorded.

Every quarter, our assistant then spends time inputting the data into QuickBooks. Some people ask us why we do not use QuickBooks. The answer is we have been using Excel since the day we opened our real estate business and as the saying goes, 'If it isn't broke, don't fix it.' We do not know the first thing about QuickBooks but we definitely know our way around a spreadsheet; this system works perfectly well for us!

The point here is that you must find an accounting/record keeping system that works for you whether it's a ledger, an Excel spreadsheet or a sophisticated piece of software. Your accountant will need to know how your funds were spent, what expenses are tax deductible, what long term and short term gains or losses you have experienced etc.

If you are one of those people who stuffs all your receipts into a shoebox and drops them off at your accountant's office, this is your wake up call to change! The more organized you are during the year, the less daunting your end of year tax filing becomes! In all honesty, if you applied for a loan and the officer asked you specific financial questions about your business, would you be able to give an answer? Questions such as how much money have you spent this year to date? Or how much do you need to sell your current investment property for to break even? There are many questions that you will not be able to answer accurately if you do not implement a solid accounting system.

Spend a few minutes each day recording your financial transactions. All of the accurate information about your budget and cash flow will be neatly organized and available at your fingertips anytime it is needed.

Need an accounting spreadsheet to get started? Visit www.101rules.com/tools now.

When Creating Budgets, Always Allow For Overruns

In real estate and life, things rarely go as planned so we always plan for the unexpected and you should too.

No matter how detailed you are with your real estate transactions, overruns commonly occur. An overrun is simply another term for going over budget. No matter how thorough you are with cost planning, it's a simple fact that you will often not be able to completely predict all of the costs of a renovation project.

For example you may be renovating a kitchen and after removing the old cabinets, you find rotten foul-smelling floorboards that are in dire need of replacement.

During a roof replacement you may find rotten wood. While replacing a window, water damage may have penetrated the studs, necessitating replacement along with dry walling, texturing, and painting. Your property might need a new paint job, new vanity units, tile repair, pool re-screening etc. The list is infinite but your budget is not.

As investors, our budgets must be vigilant and strict, however be sure to add some padding for uncalculated extra costs. While this padding is a necessity, make sure you do not go overboard with your renovations by letting your emotions take control. Remember this is a business and emotions can quickly turn a fixer-upper into a money pit.

Budget 10% to 15% for renovation overruns as this should create enough of a cushion for unexpected issues. Sometimes this extra budgeting amount isn't used while other times it is all used. If you find yourself using 20% or more of a budget, you should re-evaluate your estimating methods. Make sure your budgeting is realistic by taking a conservative approach and researching current costs.

The most important thing to remember is, whether or not you use this overrun money, always budget for it.

Know What You Can Deduct As Expenses and Maximize Them

No one likes to pay taxes but it is one of those things in life that you have to do. Like the saying goes, there are two certain things in life: death and taxes. Just because you have to pay taxes does not mean you shouldn't take full advantage of all the tax breaks that the government offers you as a business owner.

While renovating our first property, we kept a manila envelope that was used to hold all of our receipts for accounting purposes.

Other expenses such as cell phone bills, Internet bills, mileage, etc. would also be accounted for. Some items you may consider as personal can be written off, even if it is only a percentage.

You may have a section of your garage that holds equipment such as tools, paint and ladders. Keep details of how much space is being dedicated to business vs. personal usage as it could be used as a tax write off.

Your accountant can determine what is tax-deductible or not as long as you keep good records. Having poor or NO records will result in smaller or worse, no tax deductions.

THAT'S LIKE THROWING MONEY DOWN THE DRAIN!

At the time of this book the mileage tax deduction rate for business vehicles is $0.50 a mile. We drive about 20,000 miles a year *just* for business! That's $10,000 a year in deductions! YES you read that right!

We recently met a man by the name of Martin who had purchased his second investment property only three months prior. Martin was bubbling over with enthusiasm and explained how his passion for life had been reignited due to his new career as a real estate investor. Martin had been working for the local county for 20 years and was experiencing severe boredom at work. His plan was to build his business slowly in hopes of becoming a full-time real estate investor within five years. His enthusiasm reminded us of when we began investing. As we discussed his first investment property, Martin mentioned he was doing all of his own accounting and tax returns. When we explained all the possible tax deductions to Martin, he seemed quite surprised. We assumed our advice was common knowledge among business owners but it goes to show you, never make assumptions.

We explained to Martin that every penny he had spent renovating his property could be expensed against his income. This included service repairs, subcontractors, fixtures and fittings, appliances, consulting work, and many other things he had overlooked. Martin did not even know he could deduct mileage spent driving to and from his investment properties.

We advised Martin not to be cheap when it comes to accounting and to spend the money on a good accountant. He was probably losing thousands of dollars in expense tax write-offs.

We met up again with Martin a few weeks later and were pleased to learn he had taken our advice and hired a good accountant. This accountant resubmitted Martin's modified tax returns including all possible deductions. Martin's tax liability was significantly reduced and he received a substantial refund. Make sure that you follow the same advice and educate yourself on the many expenses that you can deduct on your tax return.

Don't Put All Your Eggs into One Basket

We met Jim at a local real estate investors club. He was very humble and asked if we would like to have lunch with him to share ideas; we graciously accepted.

Jim was a veteran real estate investor from Miami, Florida who had purchased his first rental property in 1982. After amassing 20 rentals and paying down the loans over a 10 year period, Jim decided to sell his portfolio and use the money to take a few years off work and travel the world. He was in a very enviable position! Jim and his wife traveled for four years visiting and residing in such countries as New Zealand, Nepal, Thailand, and Africa. Upon their return, Jim was offered a job position he could not refuse so he decided to re-enter the workforce and invest in real estate in his spare time.

Even though Jim was sitting on a large amount of capital, he was a fairly conservative investor so he was patient as he searched for an opportunity to re-enter the real estate market. Supply was scarce because at the time South Florida was experiencing a real estate boom and properties were hard to find. As more time passed, Jim became more impatient and began to look at investments he would normally not have considered.

During the real estate boom, condo conversions became all the rage. Condo conversions are apartment complexes that are converted it into saleable residential units. These apartment complexes are originally built to be rentals so the quality is usually on the cheap side. Thin walls, poor insulation and cheap fixtures are the norm.

Jim was offered a *great deal* by a developer on 15 condo conversion units. The developer told Jim that the units were already pre-sold to overseas investors and that it was a home run investment. Jim visited the condo complex, and despite noticing several issues that might cause sales difficulties, the developer convinced him that the condo conversions would be easy to resell.

Jim decided to proceed forward and paid cash for the 15 units, even though this would deplete his entire cash reserve earned from the sale of his portfolio several years earlier.

Each condo needed to be renovated and the developer provided a team of sub contractors to choose from to complete the renovations in 45 to 90 days. The renovation list was quite extensive including new kitchen cabinets and hardware, new flooring, new countertops, new light fixtures, popcorn ceiling removal, recessed lighting, and air conditioning replacement. Jim proceeded to schedule the work with the subcontractors and the renovations proceeded smoothly for the first few weeks. After that, the subcontractors began to fall behind and Jim was given many excuses and empty promises. During the renovations, Jim was losing money because he was unable to receive any rental income. As the project ran into further delays, Jim became aggravated as he watched the real estate market begin to downturn and before long, the real estate crash of 2007 occurred. Jim's project was now six months overdue and the supposed presale buyers canceled their contracts.

Eventually, the condo conversion project was completed but it was too late. The real estate market was heading in the wrong direction as property values and sales prices rapidly decreased. The buyers' market had dried up and condo conversions were no longer in demand. Jim abandoned his plan of selling the condos and was forced to rent them in the hope that the real estate market would rebound, which of course it did not. After holding the properties for two years and watching the values decrease further and further, Jim decided to cut his losses and sell them for 75% less than he had paid for them.

As we listened to Jim's story it saddened us because it was like so many other stories we have heard from other investors. People became engulfed in projects they would have normally steered clear of because of the real estate boom. This investment meant Jim had lost 75% of the portfolio capital he had worked so hard to create. If Jim had invested in one or two condos and used his remaining capital to buy other forms of real estate, he would not have found himself in this disastrous position.

When you invest in real estate it is important to start slowly and build from there. Diversifying your investments will reduce your risk should a market downturn occur. Smart people learn from their mistakes and even smarter people learn from other people's mistakes so take heed of Jim's story. Never put all of your eggs into one basket. Diversifying your real estate investments will result in you enjoying a long and prosperous career.

LOCATION, LOCATION, LOCATION...

Buy the Worst House in the Best Neighborhood

If you wish to become a real estate investor, this is one of the classic golden rules that you will need to learn and never forget. It may seem like a simple rule, but because many investors put their hearts in front of their logical minds, it's a rule that is often forgotten.

Occasionally we host neighborhood real estate education trips. We take novice investors through neighborhoods in search of potential real estate deals to get them started. Often we view houses that are in total disrepair and we are quite surprised by the negative reactions from the novice investors. Houses like this fill us with excitement!

On one occasion we were driving through a neighborhood with Wendy, a family friend who was looking to buy her first rental property. We decided to let Wendy direct us towards the homes she thought were most appealing to her. As is typical, a beautiful four-bedroom three-bathroom house captured Wendy's attention. We asked her what she liked about the house and she said that the outside really caught her eye, especially the new paint and the pretty landscaping.

We explained to Wendy that this is the last house she should consider. She looked quite surprised and asked why. We explained that since the house was in great condition and the price was high, the numbers would not work in regards to how much rent she could collect versus the mortgage amount. We also explained that buying the pretty house in the nicest neighborhood is fine for a personal residence, but not for an investment property. We then took Wendy to a dilapidated house that was tucked away at the end of a cul-de-sac. The roof was missing shingles, the siding was in need of replacement and the lawn was dying. We asked what she thought about this property and she said, "Ugh". Obviously she was not impressed.

We took an informational flyer out of the mailbox of the dilapidated house and studied the numbers. Even at the asking price, there was plenty of room to budget for renovations and if all went to plan, the amount of rent collected would far exceed the mortgage, tax and other expenses.

After explaining the numbers to Wendy, she began to see why considering the worst house in the neighborhood made sense. Wendy recognized how differently her reactions were when seeing the nice house versus the dilapidated house and realized how letting these emotions affect her decisions could be detrimental, especially financially.

Purchasing the nicest house in a neighborhood decreases your chances of seeing any major increase in appreciation. Quite the opposite is true when considering the worst house in the best neighborhood; these houses offer the greatest opportunities for profit. The worst house for sale in a neighborhood can be purchased for less money while the nicest houses command premium prices. The higher-end houses can provide you with an example of what your dilapidated house could be worth if it were brought to a comparable condition. If you overpay for the nicest house in a neighborhood and prices decrease, you will have negative equity whereas if you pay a lower amount for a fixer upper, you will have plenty of financial maneuvering room.

Nicer houses can also decline in price, especially when they are not maintained and fall into disrepair. By purchasing a higher end home, you are leaving yourself open to a huge potential downside.

By purchasing the worst house in the nicest neighborhood your upsides are plentiful so always look for the worst house in the nicest neighborhood and try to make a deal at the right price. It will be the best investment you make.

There are Gems all Around You - Learn to Read a Plat Map

This chapter is for you if you attend auctions and like finding a real gem right before your eyes! What is the point of being surrounded by gems if you can't locate them? When buying vacant land at auction, there may be times where there are mailing addresses for the property owner, but no physical vacant land address. Some investors disregard pieces of land because of a lack of a physical address and their inability to locate it. Finding the land can be as simple as using Google or your favorite search engine. Technology is a beautiful thing. We can obtain directions, find answers to problems we cannot solve ourselves and locate land without a physical address. In order to find these types of land that do not have addresses, you need to understand Plat Maps and how to read them. This chapter is very important. We use plat maps at least five or six times a year.

Properties are broken up into Townships, Ranges, Sections, and Lots. Townships are areas running north to south while Ranges run east to west. These Townships and Ranges intersect with each other like a + sign. The area where these township and ranges intersect is 36 square miles. The map is then further broken down identifying smaller parcels called Sections. These sections are numbered boustrophedonically as seen below. Each section is 1 mile by 1 mile – 640 acres each.

6	5	4	3	2	1
7	8	9	10	11	12
18	17	16	15	14	13
19	20	21	22	23	24
30	29	28	27	26	25
31	32	33	34	35	36

The Sections can be further broken down into quarters, halves, etc. 'Lots' are generally the final breakdown of the parcel.

So for example: Lot 3, SW1/4, NW ¼, Sec 20, T4S, R2W means Lot 3 in the South West quarter of the North West quarter of Section 20 in Township 4 South, Range 2 West.

In order to locate this lot on the plat map, you would look for Township 4 South and Range 2 West. These intersect each other.

Within that intersection are 36 sections so you would look for Section 20 (Sec 20).

Within that 20th section we are looking for the North West quarter.

After locating the North West quarter, it is further divided into quarters so we would then look for the South West quarter.

After that you would look for Lot 3 and bingo, you have now located your land! It may seem long and arduous but if you want a leg up on the competition, learn to read these maps. It may not happen often but when it does, you will be able to locate land that few others can.

These auction land properties can be diamonds in the rough, ready for you to seize and make BIG profits from!

You Bought a Nice House in a Declining Neighborhood, Now What?

While we always suggest you purchase the worst house in the best neighborhood you may find yourself in the opposite position.

During a real estate conference we met an investor named Tracy who had read one of our books and approached us for some advice. Tracy had purchased a nice house in a neighborhood that was quickly declining and now she was having trouble selling. She asked us if we would take a look at the house to see if we had any ideas why it was not generating any interest. Tracy was in desperate need to sell and could not continue to pay the holding costs for much longer so we agreed to meet her the following week. Pulling into the neighborhood it was blatantly obvious that her neighbors did not care about the appearance of their properties. The biggest problem was neglected, overgrown lawns that appeared as if they had been un-maintained for weeks at a time.

Tracy's house was actually the nicest in the neighborhood, which presented a problem. We always advise buying the worst house in the best neighborhood and not the other way around. There were four houses in her neighborhood that would put off potential buyers, but thankfully most of the problems appeared to be cosmetic such as paint and overgrown lawns. We came up with a plan to have Tracy fix these cosmetic problems herself. We told her to approach each neighbor and tell them she was involved in a 'neighborhood improvement initiative' and that she would mow their lawns and complete touch up paint free of charge. Each of her four neighbors were more than happy to let Tracy complete these cosmetic fixes. Tracy hired a local lawn care company to cut the lawns, and a handyman to complete the touch up paint. Everything was completed within three days. She then re-advertised her property and distributed color flyers to all the local homes and businesses. Almost immediately Tracy received an offer on her home.

If you find yourself in a similar situation, do not be afraid to take control and do whatever it takes to sell your property!

Front Landscaping is as Important as the Interior

Curb appeal, curb appeal, curb appeal! Do not ever forget these important words if you want to be a successful real estate investor.

Our investor friend Todd once called us complaining about his struggles to sell a house that he had renovated six months prior. Todd could not understand why the house was not selling as it had four bedrooms, three full bathrooms and 2600 square feet of living space sitting on a half acre lot. Todd had also painted the house and even installed a hot tub in the backyard. He asked if we would view the house to see if we had any suggestions so we agreed to meet Todd the following day. As we drove through the neighborhood, we paid special attention to the appearance of the other houses on the same street. We noticed the beautiful lush landscaping that surrounded these houses. The owners had lovingly installed palm trees, colorful flowers and plants, and lush green St. Augustine grass.

As we arrived at Todd's house we could immediately see the issues. Before we made any suggestions we decided to take a look at the interior of the house to make sure that the outside was not the only problem. Todd had done a marvelous job on the inside and the back yard was pristine. Funnily enough he had spent time and money on landscaping the backyard but completely neglected the front. Todd's thinking was that people spent much more time in the back of the house than in the front so the back yard was where he had decided to spend money. The problem for him is that most people make their house buying decision within the first minute of seeing the front of the house, so Todd's lack of attention to the front landscaping was putting off potential buyers. When we explained this to Todd, he immediately recognized his mistake and quickly installed some nice landscaping at the front of the house.

One week after landscaping the front garden, Todd received a full price offer on his home and he was ecstatic.

Always remember that the appearance of the front of a house is just as important as the interior so pay special attention to this area.

Know Your School District

Seems like a simple concept right? You are probably reading this rule thinking, "Duh that goes without saying", but this simple rule is ignored time and time again.

Buying a house in a badly performing school district can decimate your property value. It still amazes us how many investors do not bother to research the school districts using the ready available statistics. We cannot stress how important and valuable this information is, so use the tools that exist online and educate yourself.

We had just finished speaking at a local real estate investors club when a woman named Patricia approached us for some advice. Patricia had just purchased her first investment property and was very distressed. She was extremely polite but rather inexperienced when it came to real estate investing. She seemed to overlook some of the most basic concepts we assumed to be common sense.

Patricia decided to hire us to coach her through this stressful time.

She explained that two months after purchasing her first property, she received a letter stating that the house was being rezoned to a different school; an F rated one. This is disturbing news for any real estate investor. Patricia's investment property was located right on the borderline of a B rated school zone but due to the expanding population, her neighborhood was being rezoned. Patricia was distraught as she was on the verge of selling this home to a family who had stressed the importance of living in a good school district. When they discovered the house was being rezoned, they immediately withdrew their offer and Patricia struggled to find another buyer.

The sad part of this story is that this rezoning had been planned for three years so if Patricia had researched public records, she would have known this and not purchased the house. Always use the resources available to research the school district plans in any area where you plan to invest in real estate.

Found a Good Investment Property? Is it a Good Deal?

Many amateur real estate investors are so anxious to quit their jobs and become full-time real estate investors that they often overlook many expenses.

One investor we met named Sally made this very mistake on her first purchase. Sally spent months looking for a distressed house to renovate but became disheartened as she was unable to find the perfect deal. Sally began to drop her standards and raise the budget she had set aside to purchase her first house. Eventually she came across a distressed house she thought was perfect. The problem was the house was overpriced and Sally did not pay attention to the numbers. Sally's emotions had overtaken her logical thinking. The calculations Sally had made showed her that after renovations, she would be able to generate $300 positive cash flow per month.

On paper, this looked great, but Sally had missed some key expenses that would detrimentally affect her monthly cash flow. One of these key expenses was holding back part of the rent for repairs. Tenants tend to cause wear and tear on a property. As a general rule, we hold 10% of the monthly rent aside for repair costs. During the first six months, Sally's tenant managed to cause $1000 of damage which Sally was unable to recoup. Sally had also neglected to include the interest payment she was making on her personal home equity line of credit. This line of credit was used to purchase the rental property and should have been included in her expenses. Several other expenses, totaling $350 per month, were missed by Sally. This meant that instead of receiving $300 positive cash flow per month, Sally would be losing at least $50 each month! This rental property was not such a good deal after all.

When considering purchasing any real estate investment you must be very honest about your expected expenses and make sure that you include everything. You may find that the deal you thought was perfect is far from it. Our rule is to never purchase an investment property that will have negative cash flows.

Research Your Local Sex Offender Database

This rule has saved us from making some very bad real estate purchases.

While researching an upcoming real estate auction we noticed a large three-bedroom, three-bathroom condo that was particularly cheap. The condo was newly renovated and looked 'move in' ready.

When we see deals like this, the alarm bells start ringing so we always research them thoroughly. We visited the condominium complex and to our surprise, the exterior of the buildings were newly painted, the landscaping was lush and the pool area was clean and perfectly maintained. The newer model cars in the parking lot seemed to be well cared for and honestly, it was not apparent to us why this condo was being offered so inexpensively.

We proceeded to head back to our office so we could do some comparison pricing and look at recent sales of similar condos in the area. We found a strange trend especially in this particular condominium complex. Prices seem to be rapidly falling and we needed to find out why.

We then decided to check the local sex offender database and found some disturbing information. Within this condominium complex resided no fewer than five registered sex offenders. Two of the offenders resided in the SAME building as the auction condo we were interested in.

We are all for giving people second chances and fully understand that the legal system is not perfect but this was a huge problem. After speaking with investors knowledgeable with the area we discovered that condo prices had been dropping in the complex due to current owners being unable to rent to families with children. Since the auction condo was a three-bedroom unit, this meant it would probably be rented by a family with children. This could create liability issues should anything happen.

Some home owners associations have rules and regulations concerning felons and sexual offenders but this one did not.

Though the auction condo could still have been purchased and rented to someone who did not have children, we knew our target demographic was families with children so purchasing this condo seemed like a bad investment.

The laws concerning sex offenders vary from state to state but the general rule is you cannot discriminate against a sex offender by denying them housing.

Fortunately tenant decisions are not made solely on their history. If a tenant has the potential of being dangerous or problematic, that can be a good reason to deny an application. This rule does not constitute legal advice so always follow your local, state, and federal housing laws.

After we had discovered the information regarding the sex offenders, we decided it would not be wise to purchase the auction condo. If we had not checked the sex offenders' database, it is likely we would have moved forward with the purchase only to discover this information too late. That could have been a very costly mistake!

Make sure that when you consider purchasing any type of real estate, you check for both criminal and sex offenders in the neighborhood.

www.nsopw.gov is the National Sex Offender Public Website.

NEGOTIATING

That Sounds A Little High

We picked up this rule from a friend of ours and laughed when we first heard him say it. Our friend was on a phone call to a subcontractor when all of a sudden he said, "That sounds a little high." He then paused and said nothing. An uncomfortable silence ensued. Eventually the awkward silence ended and the subcontractor responded with a lower price!

Ever since then we have religiously used the "that sounds a little high" response no matter what prices are quoted and most vendors reduce their prices without us having to say anything else!

After using this rule for a while, the subcontractor's responses become somewhat predictable. They will say:

"Who else did you get a price from?"

"What price were you thinking?"

"I don't know HOW I can get it lower."

"When do you need it completed by?"

"Let me take a look at the numbers again."

If you receive pricing resistance from the subcontractor you should simply ask, "What can we do to get these numbers down?" It is a question that opens negotiation dialogue and more often than not, results in a lower price.

These two methods will save you thousands of dollars on bids and can be used in general situations outside of real estate investing. We have used this method in places such as Best Buy to receive discounts on computers and laptops. Recently we called Best Buy for a price on some new laptops for the office. When the sales representative called us back with the price we responded by saying, "That sounds a little high..." After a brief period of silence the sales rep often does a 10% discount saving us hundreds of dollars!

This rule really works, so use it often.

When Less Is More

Sometimes we are too straightforward. We get so excited when working on a real estate deal that we try to use every logical argument to convince a seller that the price we are offering is a great deal than they should accept.

Over the course of time we have learned to be more patient and allow the process to take its natural course rather than trying to use convincing tactics. Logical arguments have their place from time to time, but not every situation calls for logic and not everyone thinks like we do. Sometimes what we perceive as being logical may seem baffling to a seller. Emotions are involved, people's livelihoods are involved, and most importantly, egos are involved.

The emotional state of the seller can contribute immensely to the final selling price of the property. Some sellers will feel bulldozed if you negotiate with guns blazing telling them exactly what you would like to pay and the reason why you will only pay that amount. **Always find out why they are selling and how the sale of their property will help them**. This helps build a relationship to get you what you want - a lower price.

If the focus of the transaction is on the seller, who they are, why they are selling, how it will help them, etc., then the focus can be taken away from the asking price. Although the initial asking price is very important, the end goal of negotiating a favorable final price is most important. You have to ask questions to find out what the seller's motivation/goal for selling is and how this transaction will help them achieve their goal quickly.

Always avoid stating the 'bottom line' price that you are willing to pay for a property. Keep the transaction solely focused upon the seller and what you can do to help them. As a side note, this method usually works best with people who are selling homes that they live in, rather than on people who are selling investment real estate. This rule will not always result in a lower asking price as some sellers have a defined number in their head that they will not deviate from, but you should use the rule regardless.

If You Don't Ask, You Don't Get

This rule is a personal favorite rule of ours. During our childhood years, we were seldom confident enough to ask our fathers for things that we wanted so we would ask our mothers instead. In most cases we were told, "Ask your dad" and upon replying "But I'm afraid to ask dad," our mothers would reply, "Son, if you don't ask, you don't get." We have applied these words of wisdom to *many* elements in business, real estate and life in general.

It always amazes us during real estate transactions how much money people leave on the table, especially in regards to closing costs.

We feel slighted if money is left on the table so we soon learned opportunities to maximize our profits by reducing our costs. After all, we are in this business to make a profit.

When we purchase a property, we request the maximum amount of contributions from the seller towards the prepaids and closing costs. Depending on the type of loan (if there is a loan) on the property, some lenders have restrictions on how much a seller can contribute towards closing costs.

At the time of writing this book, if you are receiving a standard FHA loan, the maximum contributions towards closing costs by the seller is 6.0%. This means if you are purchasing a $200,000 house, the seller can contribute a maximum of $12,000 towards your pre-paids and closing costs.

Different lenders have different limits so make sure you do your homework. Some lenders will not allow the dollar amount to exceed the actual closing costs. For example if you ask for a $12,000 contribution but closing costs only total $5400, then $5400 would be the maximum amount allowed. Other lenders will allow the excess contribution amount to be paid towards closing costs and other 'prepaids'. Prepaids are items such as deposits and, appraisals, etc.

This money is cash in the bank for you so remember: if you don't ask you don't get. Imagine what you could do with an extra $12,000!

Other loans such as hard money loans do not have these limitations. Ask for 7.0% closing cost contribution and see what happens…again, if you don't ask, you don't get.

This rule of "You don't ask you, you don't get" doesn't just apply to closing costs, it applies to everything you buy.

For example, when purchasing new tile, ask for free grout. You can even do this after the price has been decided on. Do not be scared to ask because the worst that can happen is you are told "no".

Ask for free delivery when purchasing new appliances. You may not always get a firm 'yes' but we can almost guarantee more often than not, you will receive at least a discount or even something for free.

When dealing with subcontractors, there are many small and affordable upgrades that they are willing to throw in because of their low wholesale costs. One of our favorites is granite counter tops. During our first 10 projects we hired different contractors using competition to reduce their prices and our costs. At one point we were paying about $30 a square foot for granite when the going rate was $45-$50 a foot! That's a 33% savings! Not only were we getting a phenomenal deal but we would also ask them to throw in the beveled edges for free!

Generally these beveled edges would be an up-charge per linear foot and that extra cost could easily amount to $200-$300 extra per job.

So remember if you don't ask, you don't get. This rule has no limitations so use it and start saving money today!

Matt's Rule: Never Sell Past the Close

Laurence always used to joke about how much I liked to talk. When I get excited about something I like to talk about it; it's just my personality. But there was one occasion where I learnt a very valuable lesson about talking too much.

We had just completed renovating a single family home when we received a phone call from a very enthusiastic potential buyer named Pat who had seen the property while riding by on his motorcycle. Pat really liked the large garage that was built separately from the house and he explained it would be a perfect place to store his motorcycle collection. Pat had been looking for a house with a separate garage for several months but was unable to find something suitable - up until now.

We invited Pat over to the house to take a tour. He was very excited during the tour and Laurence commented to me on how the house seemed to be selling itself. As I showed Pat around I felt compelled to point out all of the different features that we had added to the house. I was very proud of this house renovation, especially the upgrades in the kitchen. I explained to Pat all the different aspects of the renovation job including some of the issues that we had run into during the demolition phase. Laurence noticed the Pat was becoming less enthusiastic the more information that I gave him, however I was just so excited about the project that I couldn't help myself.

While we were touring the living room, Pat abruptly said that he was going to have to cut the viewing short. We asked him if there was something wrong to which he replied he would have to come back at another time. Pat then abruptly jumped on his motorcycle and rode off into the distance, never to be heard from again. We could only conclude that by giving him too much information and selling past the close, I had put him off the house completely. This was a very expensive lesson to learn but now, Laurence and I are very careful not to sell past the close.

Listen and Understand

After several months of working out of a home office, we moved into a commercial office space which we found created a structured environment with fewer distractions. This did not mean we stopped working from home completely, but we did make certain days our office days where we scheduled meetings, discussed contractor bids and planned for future events.

Shortly after moving into our new office space, we watched as a large high rise was being constructed two blocks away. We shared an office with a prominent criminal attorney named Mark NeJame. Mark is a CNN Legal Analyst and can be frequently seen on CNN and Headline News giving his opinions on high profile legal cases. Not only was Mark a friend but he also became a business partner after we formed a land purchasing business together.

The newly constructed high rise could be seen from our office window - it was very impressive. The high rise's floor to ceiling glass windows offered magnificent views; it was definitely the crème de la crème of buildings and we wanted to be a part of it.

Mark had placed a contract on the entire 21st floor of the new building. This 20,000 square feet space would be used to house his expanding law practice (NeJameLaw.com). Mark offered us the opportunity to take a portion of this space for our real estate office. While this sounded idyllic, a spectacular building comes with a steep price tag. The price was $196 per square foot and that was in 'shell condition', meaning only the windows, concrete floors, ceilings, and bathrooms were included. The rest of the build-out costs and specifications would be left to Mark to shoulder.

When we met with Mark to discuss the deal, we wanted to buy 1000 square feet of the 20,000 he had contracted. Essentially we would have been 5% owner of the whole floor. It was exciting to think we were going to own part of a floor in the most sought out building in Orlando!

During the negotiations Mark explained the total floor cost including build-out was going to be about $4 million. $800,000 (20%) would be the cash down payment, and Mark would finance the remaining $3.2 million. When we discussed the terms, we calculated our part of the down payment as $40,000 or 20% of our office cost. We went on to discuss what our contribution would be to the monthly payment and other expenses. Mark explained that he would be the sole person on the loan for the $3.2 million and that since we carried little risk we would be asked to contribute a larger down payment; $80,000 instead of $40,000. We were concerned this number was too high.

We went back and forth for some time until we realized we were at an impasse. We negotiated for a smaller down payment and higher monthly payment while Mark insisted on a larger down payment and reduced monthly payments. We all had the same goals in mind but we were not seeing eye to eye on the terms and could not reach an agreement. After a couple months of discussions, our opportunity passed and we did not move into the new building.

We had lunch with Mark several weeks later and he said this: "Guys you failed to understand that what I was asking for was what I needed to complete the deal. An $800,000 down payment is a large amount of cash and your $80,000 would have helped me out greatly. You could have negotiated for no payments for several months but you failed to realize my *needs*, and cared only about your own needs."

Hearing this was rather embarrassing. We could have negotiated a deal which would have allowed us to be payment free for years but we failed to see the big picture. Mark *desired* that down payment money so he could avoid the burden of putting up so much cash. His law firm would then use its income to pay the monthly loan payments. What Mark *sought* was a contributing partner to help raise capital but we were so busy considering our own needs, we failed to see the whole picture and therefore lost an amazing opportunity. We have since applied this 'Listen and Understand' rule to many facets of our lives. When selling a home we spend extra time listening to the potential customer's *needs* and the reasons why they are looking to buy. A buyer's needs may be financial such as a low down payment or maybe they have the money for a down payment but need low monthly payments.

For example, let us imagine you are trying to sell a house that features a beautiful pool and you have found a potential buyer who has a small dog and two young children. You may assume that the yard would be ideal for the dog and the pool would be ideal for the kids, but what if your potential buyer started to talk about safety and hygiene concerns? Your sales focus should immediately change towards the built in alarm system, pool fence and warning alarm, and nearby dog park.

This type of dynamic listening and thinking also works when negotiating home prices. A woman named Gina was facing foreclosure and needed to sell her house immediately. The house had very little equity in it but the payments were very low. Gina owed $3000 in back due mortgage payments and had nowhere to turn for help. To make matters worse she had no money saved up to move so she decided it was better for her *not* pay the mortgage and live in the property for free until she could save money to rent and move.

After an hour of discussion, Gina explained why she wanted to move. Her house brought back too many bad memories. Gina had been married for 40 years when her husband unexpectedly passed away inside the house. This was a difficult experience for Gina so we agreed to pay her $2000 to leave. This gave her enough to rent a small apartment so she could begin moving with her life. Gina was very relieved to know her home was going to be receiving love and care and that it would be fixed up and sold. Gina did not have the money to move or the skills to make the repairs and the thought of being in the house during a bank foreclosure was very stressful.

When dealing with people, find out what is important to them and create mutually beneficial situations. By focusing on these wants and needs, transactions will become much easier... and you might just reach that 21st floor office space you have always dreamed of!

When Negotiating, Find Out a Seller's Motivation

Depending on whom you ask, negotiation in real estate is viewed with mixed feelings. For some people, negotiating is more painful than going to the dentist and for others, it's a joy. For us, negotiating real estate deals was uncomfortable at first but as we became more experienced, it became easier. Negotiating is a part of the real estate game that is unavoidable. We like to look at negotiating as a way of providing a win-win situation for all parties involved.

Even though we never want to take advantage of anyone in a real estate transaction, we always try to negotiate the best deal possible.

One of our first real estate deals involved us negotiating with an older gentleman named Jerry. At first appearance, Jerry seemed abrasive and had a concrete plan for selling his home. He was adamant that no one would lowball him as he had a price in his mind and he would not reduce the price by even a penny. The issue here was that Jerry's asking price was far too high. His house needed expensive repairs including septic tank removal, plumbing repairs, electrical updates, and a new roof. Jerry thought he would be able to sell his home at market value without taking into account these repairs but quickly found out that no one would pay his asking price.

Normally we would have given up on this negotiation due to the tough stance of the seller, but we liked the house as it was located in a great neighborhood and would make a perfect rental property. We had been searching for a house in this very neighborhood for several months but inventory was scarce. After an hour of negotiating it seemed we had hit a brick wall. Here we were trying to explain why we should get the house at a certain price while Jerry was digging his heels in, adamantly rejecting our offer.

Just as we were about to give up, Jerry received a phone call from his daughter. After the phone call ended, Jerry seemed visibly upset. We asked Jerry if anything was wrong and he explained that his daughter had just had surgery and that he needed to relocate in order to look after her family whilst she was recovering.

Now we knew that Jerry's motivation for selling was to be close to his daughter, we were able to communicate with him in a far more effective manner.

We explained to Jerry that we could close on his home quickly with cash so he would be able to move much faster than if he were to sell his home to someone going through the mortgage application process. We also offered to pay for his moving expenses. Hearing this, Jerry softened and we were able to negotiate a price which worked for both of us.

Make sure when you are negotiating real estate deals you focus on the seller and what their needs and motivations are. By diverting the focus away from yourself, you will close far more deals.

Any Percentage of a Deal Is Better Than Zero

When analyzing a deal, it is always tempting to look for the maximum amount of money you *could* make; however in some cases it is better just to make a small amount of profit rather than no profit.

There are times when we become involved in multiple simultaneous deals where our financial resources become limited. On one such occasion, a seller named Luis who desperately needed to move due to a job change offered to sell us his home. His job change involved an overseas relocation and Luis did not want the hassle of renting and managing his home from a distance. Luis had plenty of equity in his home and was quite happy to sell for a big discount as long as the transaction could be completely quickly. Luis made it clear he would not agree to a contract with an assignment clause as he did not want anything to delay the sale.

Buying this home would have been a big stretch for us and we did not want to put ourselves into a financial bind. We decided to make some phone calls and offer the deal to some of our local investor associates. Many of our associates were also low on financial resources but after a few days we were able to find someone who was very interested in the deal.

We offered the interested investor a partnership deal but he did not want any partners and was only interested in paying a referral fee. We then tried negotiating a split percentage with the investor because we knew there was a lot of equity in the home. We also knew time was not on our side and that the seller, Luis, was talking to other potential buyers. The bottom line was that we had to close on the deal immediately.

We eventually settled on a 2% referral fee calculated on the final sales price. Two percent is less commission than a real estate agent would generally receive if they had listed the property and sold it. (Generally two agents would split 6%, 3% for each agent.)

All parties were happy with the deal because it provided a win-win solution. Luis was ecstatic to have sold his home so quickly for cash. We were happy to receive a small referral fee for making a few phone calls and the best part: we had zero financial risk.

It would have been very easy for us to tell the seller we were not interested and to continue on with our other projects, but instead, a little creative thinking resulted in a situation that benefited all parties involved.

When you become an experienced investor, there may be times where you find many great deals but lack the financial resources to complete them all. Too many deals you say? Yes, it does happen. Money and capital will always run out before the deals do.

If you are ever faced with a situation where you can make a small amount of money by assigning a contract or referring a property to another investor, you must take that opportunity as making a small percent on the deal is far more beneficial than making zero percent.

Never Count Other People's Money!

The first time we heard this saying we had no idea what it meant or why we were being told it. It turned out to be one of the best pieces of advice that we have ever received.

Our friend Mark is a very successful criminal attorney. Mark has defended some very high profile people on national, international and federal levels. You may have seen some of his cases on the national media. Needless to say Mark is very intelligent and whenever he speaks or offers advice, we listen!

On one occasion we were having dinner with Mark while discussing a dilemma. Our dilemma was that we were being offered a partnership in a real estate deal where we would receive a far smaller percentage than the person who was offering it to us. The deal would still be lucrative even at this low percentage rate, but our minds were solely focused on how much of a larger percentage the other party would receive. After we were finished venting our grievances to Mark, he delivered some phenomenal advice:

"What does it matter how much the other party is making? You will both benefit immensely from this deal so stop focusing on what you're not making and most importantly - stop counting other people's money!"

At first Mark's words did not make sense! Of course we were interested in how much the other party was making because without us, they could not complete the deal. Our mental roadblock was that after we knew how much our new partner was going to make, it made our portion seem small and insignificant. Ego and greed were mentally crippling and hindering us from completing the deal.

The deal was beneficial to both parties involved and we would have been fools to pass it up but we almost felt as if we were being taken advantage of. The reality was that neither one of us could complete the deal without each other.

After some contemplation time, Mark's comments seemed to sink in and since that day we have always heeded his advice.

It makes no sense to focus on what other people are making financially; that is their business. As long as you are comfortable being involved in a deal that is mutually beneficial, focus on yourself and do not let greed and ego get in the way.

In our deals, we now choose to focus on the benefits we receive. This leads to happy, resentment-free working relationships. It does not matter whether we are earning a small percentage or a large percentage; we have learned to be happy with what we are earning and to also be happy for the other people involved too.

Our rule is not suggesting that a real estate deal should always favor one person or the other. Instead we suggest you enter into deals that are fair to all people involved and that you focus on making certain you:

1   Like the terms of the real estate deal.

2   Are appropriately compensated for the deal.

3   Your risk to reward is acceptable.

A change in attitude can go a long way. Ego, resentment and greed are like a cancer that can eat away at you. Be sure to stay positive, focus on your part of the deal and never count other people's money.

SALES AND MARKETING

Price Your Properties According to the Current Market!

This is a true story about our dear friend Tommy who is *very* successful but sometimes gets a little greedy (*sorry Tommy but we said we would write about you some day!*)

Tommy likes to buy Tax Deed properties at auctions. A Tax Deed is a property auctioned and sold by the county in order to recoup back-owed real estate taxes. Generally these properties sell for *well* below market price because the transactions must be paid for in cash within 24 hours of the sale. The lack of financing options makes these Tax Deed sales far less competitive than Foreclosure auctions. One day Tommy was at a Tax Deed auction and managed to pick up a great deal on a 1650 square foot house. The house had three bedrooms, two bathrooms, a two-car garage, and was located close to the major Orlando Florida attractions. This was a great starter home that could be sold to a landlord as a rental property or to someone looking for a primary residence or vacation property.

We were very impressed that Tommy paid the correct amount money on this home as sometimes he had a history of overpaying or as we like to call it, 'auction fever'. This was Tommy's second property and if he played his cards right, he was due to make a healthy profit. There was only one problem. Tommy became greedy and listed the property for $232,900. This property's market value was much closer to $205,000 based on a market price of $124 per square foot. The $124 per square foot pricing would almost certainly lead to a quick sale.

We tried to explain to Tommy that he was over pricing his property by more than $27,000 and that this would eliminate many of the entry-level buyers. Due to the high price point, Tommy's starter home was entering the mid level price bracket usually reserved for nicer homes with more features, located in higher end neighborhoods. Tommy would not listen and his $27,000 over pricing mistake resulted in zero offers - no one was interested.

If you do not get offers on a property in the first three or four weeks, you might have to re-evaluate your price to make sure it is in-line with the market value of comparable houses. It took almost three months for Tommy to realize his error and reduce his price to $205,000, a price much closer to its actual value. Unfortunately when a house sits for too long on the market and then experiences a major price reduction, real estate agents and potential buyers see this as a sign of desperation. In this case they were right; Tommy was running short of cash and was desperate to sell!

We truly felt bad for Tommy but we had tried to warn him about his pricing methods and now he was paying the price. Tommy's mistakes were costly in four ways:

1.   He lost money on interest payments for the extra months the property remained unsold.
2.   He lost opportunities on other houses he could have purchased with his tied up capital.
3.   His profit was reduced from having to accept a desperation offer, which was lower than the price the house should have sold for.
4.   He lost money paying for extra utilities, insurance, taxes, and marketing costs

At the end of the day Tommy still made a profit but this profit was less than he *could* have made, Tommy learned a valuable lesson the hard way and now he prices his properties slightly under the current market value in order to sell quickly.

Don't pull a 'Tommy' and make sure you choose the correct listing price on your properties. By doing so you ensure the best situation for a quick sale by minimizing costs, profits and freeing up your capital to pursue other deals.

Your Properties must be a Cut above the Rest

Most investment properties or fixer uppers are not palatial properties with the name 'Trump' plastered on them. We do not have a brand name associated with our properties so we have to use other methods to invoke fast sales.

It is common knowledge that the two areas where you should concentrate most of your renovation efforts are the kitchen and the bathrooms. Money spent in these two areas can vastly improve the attractiveness and value of a home. According to houselogic.com, a kitchen renovation could net 72% in return, meaning a $20,000 kitchen investment could result in a $14,000+ increase in your sales price. This depends on other factors such as comparable house prices and whether or not your potential buyers appreciate the increased value of a nice kitchen. As a general rule of thumb, the lower grade the home, the lower the return on the renovation investment and vice versa.

In regards to bathrooms, according to Money.Cnn.com, the return on investment on a mid-range bath modernization is 102% of its cost. Outdated bathrooms are very common in older first time homes so renovating these areas is a great way to enhance your property value. What if your budget doesn't allow for major kitchen and bath remodels and you considered these areas to be acceptable? There are some simple upgrades to spice up these and other areas such as:

Install granite counter tops.

Upgrade appliances or install stainless steel or black appliances

Install crown molding.

Install a rain style showerhead.

Install high quality drawer handles and knobs.

Install tile mosaic backsplashes.

Install high quality landscaping, remember quality not quantity.

Pick your upgrades wisely and always stay on budget. Be sure to choose upgrades that will have the most impact on the buyer and create the quickest sales.

Include Financing Numbers in Your Flyers and Advertising

This simple rule is vital and extremely effective. It is also one we did not incorporate when we began our real estate investing careers. Many times potential buyers do not believe they can afford to buy a home, however a simple written explanation explaining the numbers can show them otherwise.

One of our first home renovations projects was located in a friendly community style neighborhood. We had become quite friendly with an older gentleman named Ronnie and would always chat with him for a few minutes while taking a break from hammering nails. Once we had completed the renovation project, we held an open house to garner some interest. After a quiet open house, Ronnie wandered in to say hello. We were quite surprised to learn he had lived by himself in the same rented house for 15 years; we had always assumed he owned the house. We always encourage owning rather than renting, however some people do not want the maintenance and expense that come with home ownership. Others are simply unaware that they can afford to buy rather than rent.

Upon learning that Ronnie had rented for so long, we handed him our sales flyer and showed him how much it would cost him to own our home. He was paying $1100 per month in rent and was quite surprised to learn than he could own our newly renovated house for only $900 per month due to the low interest rates being offered by the bank. Our sales flyer clearly explained the estimated monthly payment (including taxes and insurance). We also included estimated payment differences for people with great, average and poor credit. It transpired that Ronnie had excellent credit making his monthly payment more than affordable. Ronnie purchased our home and four weeks later, he moved out of his 15 year rental home.

This simple rule of including financing plans on sales flyers will enable you to sell your properties much easier. For sales flyer templates visit www.101rules. com/tools

Stay Educated and Current with Open Houses

Using the Internet, you can enter addresses into a search engine and find photos of properties for sale, neighborhood statistics and comparable home values. This information is great to help guide you in marketing and sales but it should not be your only resource.

Open houses are often overlooked as a source of information for neighborhoods and comparable properties. During our first two years in real estate we were so focused on buying, fixing and selling that we lost sight of what was going on around us. We did plenty of online research but our agent pointed out that we were missing out on other aspects that could help our home sales.

Our real estate agent Pat recommended that we spend a weekend researching comparable properties within a two-mile radius of where our own homes were located. We agreed and asked Pat to email us a list of property addresses from the MLS (Multiple Listing Service database) so we could research them online. Pat responded, "No, you're going to DRIVE to these properties during the open house times and look inside them." We really did not want to do this but Pat had never given us bad advice so we reluctantly set off to view the list that he had compiled for us.

After visiting two open houses, we started to see some of the things we could have been doing better. Encouragingly, we also saw some areas in which we were miles ahead.

The open houses showed us which areas of repairs and improvements we were doing right and wrong. For example, Pat showed us a property online being sold by an investor who appeared to have built high quality custom book shelves inside the family room. When we actually saw the family room, it was apparent the investor owner had nailed some cheap store-bought shelving to the wall. Now do not get us wrong, we have bought accent pieces from value furniture stores and there is nothing wrong with that but this house though was filled with these cheap add-ons that were intended to look like custom furniture. Other people who were there for the open house were obviously put off by the poor decor as they were not staying for very long.

On the flipside, we saw some creative features at this particular home. The investor had created a unique tile medallion as a centerpiece around a lighting fixture in the dining room. The cost effective medallion made the chandelier a centerpiece of the room and was very impressive.

While you can buy countless design magazines to spark your inspiration, nothing can beat visiting open houses and seeing how other people prepare their homes for sale. Visit as many open houses as you can, especially ones that are within the vicinity of any property you are trying to sell. It will help you create a better product and avoid making mistakes other sellers are making.

Always Have a Full Color Flyer Listing the Comparable Values for Your Property

We now live in a culture where people base their decisions on looks. The more eye-catching and aesthetically pleasing something is, the more it likely it is to sell. Just look at the graphics on laundry detergent bottles and cereal boxes! How about cars? We are a society so engulfed in looks that we judge a car purchase based on its exterior styling even though the interior mechanics and engine might be subpar. The same holds true with real estate and its advertising. The nicer it looks, the easier it sells.

Back in our early investing days, we purchased and renovated a pretty three-bedroom, two-bathroom cottage house. While the cottage was adorable, it did not have any drive-by traffic since it was located at the end of a cul-de-sac. It would take strong advertising methods to sell the cottage quickly in order to avoid expensive holding costs. We started by designing a simple black and white flyer and distributed it to all the local neighbors, stores and agents offices. After not receiving a single phone call for a whole week, we knew something in our marketing technique was not working. We decided drastic measures were needed so we drove through the neighborhood looking at other homes for sale. We noticed a couple of houses offering flashy full-page color sales flyers. The flyers were so nice even *we* wanted to buy their houses.

We also noticed that most flyers included comparable values (or comps) for other sold homes in the area, something we had not thought to include in our ads. We immediately called a graphic designer and revamped our ad. Our new flyers were bright and inviting, making sure to include clear photographs and recent comparable values from recent sales in the neighborhood. As soon as we distributed the updated sales flyer, the calls started flooding in and an offer was soon received.

Spend the extra money and always use full color flyers with comparable values! For sales flyer templates visit www.101rules.com/tools

Use a Professional Photographer

Sometimes when browsing real estate listings on the Internet, it still amazes us how poor some of the photographs of the houses are. Some agents are trying to sell $250,000 properties using a $50 digital camera. What are they thinking?

You would be mistaken for thinking that photographic quality makes little difference to the amount of interest you receive on a home. In one example, an investor named Mike handed us a flyer that contained photographs of a condo he had been trying to sell for more than a year. Mike could not understand why the condo was not receiving any interest. The photos on the flyer were dark and blurry and he even had these atrocious photographs listed on the MLS. You only have one chance to make a good impression and by listing these homes with such terrible photographs, Mike had missed his chance.

We suggested to Mike that he pay a professional photographer to take quality photos of the condo he had for sale. Mike asked us what this would cost to which we responded, "Well it depends. You usually get what you pay for in the photography industry." Mike thought about it for a second then shunned our idea saying he did not want to spend the money on something that he could do himself. Mike struggled to physically see the difference between his photos and professional photos and he certainly could not see the value of good photography

We asked Mike if he had considered that his photos might be the reason for the lack of interest on his condo. Mike dismissed this idea and blamed the lack of interest on the slow moving real estate market.

Several months passed before we ran into Mike again. We asked him if he had had any success selling his properties and sadly he responded, "None at all." We once again suggested to Mike that his photographs might be the problem. We told Mike that if he could not get people into his condo to view it because of the photographs, then he would have little or no chance of making a sale. This time the message appeared to be sinking in and Mike asked if we knew any good photographers. We were happy to refer him to a local newspaper reporter who had opened a side business photographing real estate. Mike asked if we would attend the photo shoot and two weekends later, we attended Mike's first real estate photo shoot.

The photographer prepped every room in the condo making sure it was clutter free. An extensive lighting set-up was brought in since the condo was a little dark (good lighting set ups are key to achieving quality real estate photographs).

At the end of the shoot, the photographer showed Mike his old photographs alongside the new ones. Mike was truly shocked when he saw the difference and has been using this photographer ever since. Mike also received an offer on his condo three weeks later.

When trying to sell or rent your home, hire a professional photographer and make sure he or she has extensive lighting knowledge as without good lighting, you are wasting your time.

Remember that some potential buyers make a decision on a property after viewing a single photo for only a few seconds. Those are important seconds so make sure your photos are of a high quality.

Leave the Website Building to the Professionals

There is a vast difference between an amateur website and a professionally built website - we learned this the hard way.

One afternoon we were attending a business lunch with Sam, a real estate investor whom we really admired. During the meeting, we asked Sam what it would take for him to partner up with us on some deals to which he responded by asking us for our website address. Sam then pulled out his laptop and visited our website. He asked us if we thought our website was 'adequate'; we could tell he was not impressed. We never really thought too much about the quality of our website as we utilize so many different marketing techniques; however Sam explained that a company's website is the new business card. Sam's theory was that if a company's website lacked a professional appearance, it could be to the detriment of real estate sales. This theory made perfect sense.

After reviewing our website that evening, we agreed with Sam and decided to hire our own in-house website designer. Our designer completely revamped the site and gave it a fresh professional look. We couldn't believe the difference! We showed the new website to Sam and his positive reaction was gratifying. He explained that now he would be much more comfortable partnering with us on real estate deals. Sam's change of heart was based upon the fact we took his advice seriously showing that we were willing to make changes for the better.

In the months to come we experienced an increase in website traffic, leads and sales. We began to rely less on the MLS (Multiple Listing Service) and real estate agents as we began to sell more of our real estate through our website. The investment in a new website saved us tens of thousands of dollars in agent commissions. Building your own website may seem like a smart cost cutting move, however we recommend you let the professionals handle this end of your business and hire a web designer to build you a beautiful website.

For web design, we recommend www.broadstonemedia.com.

Sell Payments, Not Prices

We love car dealership commercials. Have you noticed that their commercials have a consistent formula? It's a formula that has not changed in years. Car dealerships spend thousands of dollars a month on advertising and are expert marketers. One of the first things a car salesman asks a potential customer is, "What monthly payment can you afford?"

During the slower real estate market times where inventory was high and buyers were scarce, we were forced to be creative with our marketing techniques. We experimented with the techniques dealerships use to sell cars. One of the lower-priced homes we marketed was not receiving much interest because there were so many homes for sale in the same neighborhood. After two months without receiving a single offer we decided to market the property using a monthly payment technique rather than focusing on the sales price.

No one else was doing this at the time and some investors thought we were crazy. During an open house we printed flyers which only contained monthly payment information for three categories, average credit, good credit and excellent credit. Each category listed an estimated monthly payment for what a potential buyer could expect to pay depending on their credit score. These flyers were used during our open houses.

We even removed the price of the home from all of our print advertisements and signs. This technique increased our open house traffic by 127% and the number of inquiries we were receiving from serious buyers increased too.

During one of our open houses, a man named Frank approached us waving one of our flyers while explaining he had no idea that he would be able to afford the home we were showing. We sat down with Frank and discussed the possible monthly payment scenarios, and even with his credit score being average, our house was in an affordable payment range for him. Frank said that if he had only paid attention to the sales price, he would not have even considered buying the home. The home was not overpriced but Frank lacked home buying experience and had no idea how to calculate his monthly payment. Simply put, the total home price intimidated Frank and he needed to be shown that he could purchase the home on an affordable plan.

Chatting with Frank we realized how it important it was to list monthly payment information on our flyers. We continue to use this marketing technique for every property we sell.

We found that in most cases, people are more interested in the monthly payment information rather than the total home price. This was something that we had completely overlooked.

Using the 'Sell Payments, Not Prices' techniques on your own real estate deals can help sales, particularly in slow market times.

Bathrooms and Kitchens Sell the House!

When we renovate houses, we pay special attention to certain areas that will help to sell the house quickly.

One summer we were driving through a neighborhood and spotted a house that was *For Sale by Owner*. The house looked extremely neglected and even the For Sale sign was cracked and faded which indicated it had been vacant for quite some time. Some investors steer clear of these projects viewing them to be to be ugly and time consuming but we see these houses as an opportunity. As Warren Buffett says, "Dive into markets no one else wants to dive into." This is a concept you should always remember when investing in real estate.

We called the owner of the neglected house and arranged a viewing time. Once we entered the house we could see exactly why it had remained unsold for so long. The kitchen was very small, the layout was not functional and the bathrooms smelt terrible. These two things alone would put most buyers off, especially if they are female.

The owner of the property was anxious to sell and offered us a deal we could not pass up. At the price he offered, we would have plenty of money to spend on a kitchen and bathroom overhaul so we decided to proceed forward.

During the renovation, we replaced the cabinets, countertops, sinks, faucets, light switches, power outlets, and lighting fixtures. Most importantly we reconstructed the layout of the kitchen to make it open and more functional. The difference was night and day and even now, this project remains one of our proudest. During construction, we watched this house turn from an ugly duckling into a beautiful home; a home we hoped someone would enjoy for the rest of their lives.

As we were outside laying the new grass, a car pulled into the driveway. A younger man climbed out of the car and introduced himself to us. His name was Tim and he explained that his wife had just had a new baby and that they were looking for a larger home. We invited Tim to come and take a look inside the house. As Tim looked around the home we expected him to be as excited about it as we were, and while he seemed to like the house, he did not show as much enthusiasm as we would have liked.

When we asked him his thoughts, Tim said it was very nice but he really wanted a 'man cave'. In case you do not know what this is, a man cave is a space typically filled with man toys such as a pool table, home theater or bar. Our house did not have such an area even though there was plenty of space to create one.

Tim said he would talk to his wife and ask her if she would like to come and view the house. As he left we did not think we would hear from him again. Three days later, we received an unexpected phone call from Tim asking if he could come to see the house with his wife Lisa. When Lisa saw the property for the first time, her eyes lit up and we could tell she was truly excited. The areas that we had paid special attention to were the ones that truly impressed her. Lisa loved the stainless steel appliances, open kitchen plan, recessed lighting, and the beautiful granite countertops. The kitchen alone sold Lisa on the house.

Four hours later, Tim and Lisa returned with a written offer in hand. Lisa loved the house so much their offer was at full price and they closed 30 days later. We were quite surprised at the turnaround since Tim seemed so intent on buying a house with a ready-made 'man cave'. We now understand that the woman rules the roost and that focusing on improving the kitchen and bath areas helps sell houses. When looking for real estate deals, pay special attention to making these areas shine.

Kitchens and bathrooms can make the difference between a house sitting unsold for months and receiving an offer before the paint has had a chance to dry.

It's Time to Enter the Next Stage

During the real estate boom it was extremely easy to sell houses, especially ones that had been renovated and looked nice. Selling was usually as simple as putting a For Sale sign in the front yard, having an open house and placing flyers on the kitchen countertop.

When the real estate market declined in 2007, there was a huge increase in the supply of houses for sale. This meant that as the inventory increased and the buyers decreased, the market became far more competitive and it was much more difficult to sell houses. While some investors thought it necessary to cut back on their advertising budgets, we knew that in order to sell our inventory of houses we would have to do the opposite. This was a scary time since spending more money was definitely not something we had planned on, but it was necessary.

After struggling to sell one of our renovated homes, we decided to ask some friends to take a walk through and give as their opinions. The feedback we received was that our friends could not envision what our empty house would look like with furniture in it. After two other walk-throughs, we found the feedback consistent; people had no vision of what our 'home' would look like furnished.

We then decided to stage all of our homes. Staging is often used in homebuilders' model homes to present a vision to potential buyers of how an empty house could be turned into their home. We purchased staging furniture including couches, dining room tables, area rugs, candles, coffee makers, bookcases, beds, dressers, artificial plants, and even a fake flat screen television. We turned our 'house' into a 'home' and after a few weeks, we finally we received an offer. If you own multiple properties that you are attempting to sell, consider purchasing your own staging supplies. If you prefer to rent these supplies, there are companies that specialize in staging houses.

Home staging is essential especially in a down market so make sure you calculate this into your budget.

Upgrades Galore Equals Profits No More!

Many real estate investors believe they can renovate a low-end property using high end specifications to help rejuvenate a bad area of town. This is extremely risky and rarely works so we suggest you renovate accordingly. Go with the sure bet, not the long shot.

That's not to say there aren't good real estate deals in lower end areas and we certainly are not suggesting you only purchase deals in the 'best' areas of town… most investors cannot afford the 'best' areas. Always remember the location, location, location, location rule as a reminder to try to purchase real estate in desirable areas.

We try to match the repairs, décor, landscaping, and marketing to the location. The rule for us is merely a reminder to stay grounded in our expectations of our sales price, time to move the property, upgrades, required repairs versus wanted repairs, etc.

Formica tops in a luxurious high rise in the heart of downtown?

No way!

Granite tops with beveled edges in the bathrooms of a blighted area? Bad idea!

Do we put Brazilian Cherry Hardwood in a lower end rental property? Absolutely not!

Should we install $0.69 Ceramic tile in a prestigious high rise?

Of course not!

We could give example after example but the concept is the same. Match your property to the area. Upgrades are great and essential to keep you ahead of other listings and rentals. Just remember not to overdo the upgrades as there is a point of diminishing returns where the extra amount invested will not turn into returned dollars in your pocket!

Familiarize Yourself with the Upgrades That Are Inexpensive but Look Expensive

When purchasing investment properties in need of renovation, it is very easy to make emotional decisions rather than ones that make sound financial sense. We have been in several situations where our budget was small but our ideas were big. We always try to go above and beyond to make our houses as nice as possible for the future buyer, no matter whether our budget is large or small.

Having limited renovation budgets forced us to become creative and look for ways to add the sizzle without the cost of the steak. During one of our renovations, we uncovered some unplanned repairs while demolishing a wall. We discovered that the electrical and plumbing work in the house needed to be completely replaced leaving us little money to complete the rest of the house. We had originally planned to re-paint the interior and exterior but were no longer able to do this. Instead we completed inexpensive upgrades including:

Adding ceiling fans

Replacing electrical wall plates

Replacing faucets

Touching up paint including baseboards

Replacing hardware (drawer handles etc.)

Replacing light fixtures

Cleaning up the landscaping

Repairing and cleaning the appliances

These simple upgrades can be easy on your wallet and very easy on a potential buyer's eyes. If you know where to shop, you can buy these upgrades inexpensively.

Websites such as eBay, Overstock and Amazon offer amazing deals on items that will drain your wallet if you buy them at the big hardware stores.

If you find yourself running on a tight budget for your renovation project, look for ways to add inexpensive upgrades that will make your property shine.

If People Are Hungry, Start Baking Bread

In America the geographical area is vast and very different from town to town and city to city. It is important to pay special attention to the demands in your particular market.

For example, in the downtown areas of metropolitan cities it can be far more cost effective to live in a townhouse or condo versus a single family home. Knowing this, you can focus on finding investment deals within the condo market with the assurance that there will be a strong supply of tenants. This is one of our common sense rules that some people fail to follow.

We have a family friend named Kenny who lives in Phoenix Arizona. After 25 years of toiling away as a high school teacher, Kenny was offered an early retirement package. With more time on his hands than he knew what to do with, Kenny decided to try his hand at buying and selling real estate. He repeatedly called us for starting advice stating he could not make up his mind between four different single family homes in residential neighborhoods.

After doing some research we found Kenny lived very close to Tempe, the home of Arizona State University with a student base of over 72,000. We suggested to Kenny that he look for a four or five-bedroom single family home located near the University campus. That way, instead of collecting $1200 in rent for a whole house, he could rent by the room and net up to $2500 per month. After further research, Kenny found there was a huge demand for rental houses near the University campus.

Kenny was able to find two single family homes side by side that were badly neglected and in desperate need of repair. These houses were ideal as they were located within three miles of the Arizona State University campus. Kenny was extremely handy and had a good mind for design so he created a plan to fully maximize the house living spaces.

To start with, Kenny 'student proofed' each house paying special attention to the local tenant laws. He made sure there was adequate fire protection and installed a basic fire sprinkler system. He also converted the houses from four to five bedrooms by utilizing some of the extra living room space.

Kenny was once a student himself and remembered how messy and neglectful he was, so he replaced the carpets with ceramic tile. Knowing privacy would be a big selling point, Kenny installed bedroom door locks complete with electronic key codes. He also converted the living room into a common area that would house workspace desks, power outlets and a fast wireless internet connection.

Finally Kenny created an inexpensive outdoor community area that could be used by residents of both houses. This proved to be a big hit with the students as he received many compliments stating how no other rental houses provided such nice features.

Kenny's rental agreement required a parent or guardian to provide a personally guaranteed automatic payment on the first of every month. This considerably reduced his risk of nonpayment.

When the houses were finished, Kenny sent us photos and we were truly impressed how he had paid special attention to market demands.

If Kenny had pursued his original idea of purchasing and renting to a single family, he would not have benefited from nearly the same amount of financial return. The student rooms rented in a matter of days and the houses were kept in good order as the residents were proud to live there. Kenny continued to receive rental applications and even built up a six-month waiting list. His waiting list grew so large that he purchased two other homes on the same street which he plans to convert to student housing.

If you pay special attention to the supply and demands of the areas you are focusing on, you will be able to create new markets and fulfill demands. This can be very lucrative.

Search eBay for Items for Your Houses

The Internet has truly revolutionized the way we do business in all aspects. It is difficult to envision how we managed without this resource 20 years ago. Shopping has become so much easier now.

Many years ago, a private individual named Marcus was interested in hiring us to design and build a large custom home. This home was to be two-stories, 4000 square feet of living space and feature a beautiful oasis pool. Marcus was very particular about fittings and fixtures but he was also very budget-conscious. Staying under budget during custom home building can be challenging due to the clients extravagant design ideas. This was the problem we were facing with Marcus.

Marcus informed us that no matter what happened he would not exceed the budget, not even by a dollar. This forced us to be creative and we spent hours shopping on the Internet for fixtures and fittings in order to save money. At the end of the project we realized we needed handles for all the kitchen cabinets and drawers; however our budget was completely used up. The owner had specified wanting six inch stainless steel handles which were proving to be rather expensive, especially at the local hardware stores.

We spoke with the Marcus again and explained our dilemma but he was unwilling to provide any more money. Now it was time to shift into creative mode and turn to eBay. We occasionally used eBay to buy small personal items such as books and movies but had never really looked at buying house fixtures. While browsing eBay, we were able to find beautiful items and fixtures for our new house for ridiculously low prices. Even the six inch stainless steel handles that were $20 each at a local hardware store were being offered for less than $2! There were over 60 handles in this house. This one transaction saved us over $1080!

We came to learn that eBay sells more than just your everyday clothing items and electronics. Use eBay to save thousands of dollars on everything you need for your renovations project.

Use Social Media Websites to Promote Your Products

We live in the age of technology. Many of you may be reading this book on your computer, tablet, or phone. The days of the brick and mortar stores are becoming a thing of the past. This is also true for marketing and how we reach new potential clients.

In the information society we live in and due to websites such as Google, Twitter and Facebook, your marketing should know no bounds.

We always create separate social media accounts for our businesses so our personal lives are not intertwined. An active social media marketing campaign can quickly attract potential clients, saving you thousands on real estate commissions, both on the buy and the sell side.

We have had situations where we searched Twitter for the word 'rent' and were able to rent a condo within three days instead of the usual three weeks.

How much did using Twitter to advertise our condo save us? The condo rented for just under $1000 a month, over $33 a day. If we had advertised on a rental website we may have had to discount our first month's rent and pay the advertising fee which would total anywhere from $700 to $1200.

Remember, it is not just about posting information about properties you own. It's also about *searching* these sites to find people who are looking for places to rent, services they offer, services you need, etc. Use keyword searches to find these people. These services are free with no usage limit so use these tools immediately and put them to good use!

RENTALS

Complete a Background Check on EVERY Tenant

We have rented to countless tenants and during the early days we wish we could tell you they were all model tenants! Unfortunately like most real estate investors, we have handled our fair share of evictions, poorly maintained residences, domestic issues, noise complaints, and well, too many problems to list!

After several months of these repeated situations, we decided to examine our rental practices and procedures. We soon discovered why we were having this streak of bad tenants. *WE* were the problem! It was difficult to admit at first but since there was no one else to blame, we made a prompt decision to correct our rental practices and procedure immediately.

Our first major implementation was the use of background checks. It did not matter how sweet the old couple appeared or how polite the young college student was, we made sure each tenant went through the check. Once we started completing thorough background checks, 95% of our tenant problems simply disappeared!

The checks exposed felonies, past evictions, drug arrests, battery, violence issues, etc. Even when we put on the application 'NO FELONS', felons would still apply.

We suggest charging an application fee of $100 to cover background checks. (Make sure your local laws allow this). Explain this fee to the applicant and explain the possible reasons why they would be denied acceptance. We are still amazed at the number of people who apply for a rental property even after we disclose what would cause an immediate application denial. Some applicants believe they can slip through the cracks since most landlords do not perform adequate checks.

Visit our website www.101rules.com/tools for our recommendations on background checks.

Be Sure Your Deposit Covers all Carpet Damages and Repairs

The stories we hear concerning the unimaginable conditions tenants leave vacated rental properties in never ceases to amaze us. Normal wear and tear will always occur on a rental property, no matter how good the tenant is. We find most renters do not care for the property they are residing in for one reason.... *the property is not theirs*. Most tenants view rental properties as a temporary housing situation, which is why renters move so frequently. In rare cases, we have tenants who experience pride of ownership and take very good care of their rental properties, but these cases are few and far between.

Deposits for properties need to be a realistic amount to keep the tenant applications flowing. Some states limit the amounts you can collect for deposits and require you to keep this deposit in a separate bank account so be sure to check your local laws.

If you are going to advertise a 'move in special', we suggest you keep your deposit at the normal amount and discount your 1st month's rent. For example, a typical rent plus first months would be $2000 total. If we were running a 'move-in' special on this property, we would still require the $1000 deposit and perhaps discount the 1st month's rent by 50% making the total $1500.

Never discount the deposit because you have no recourse in the event you need to carry out repairs after the tenant vacates. Repairs can be expensive and time consuming: pet damages and stains, holes in walls, plumbing neglect, odor removal, carpet burns, water damage, door knobs missing, etc. You will need all your deposit money should you need to carry out any of these repairs. Background checks and interviews help weed out potentially troublesome tenants. Remember that most laws favor the tenant so always verify your local laws regarding rental leases and make sure you write your lease and deposit rules appropriately to avoid future legal problems. If you need help with your rental contracts see our contracts at www.101rules.com/tools

A Potential Tenant's Car Will Tell You Everything

Over our years of renting we discovered one simple indicator of a future tenant's behavior. We once met a young couple that was interested in renting a three-bedroom, two-bathroom condo. They seemed very friendly and on the outside, looked to be perfect potential tenants. Since the couple was young, we asked them to provide two months of rent in advance and a security deposit, to which they happily agreed.

Soon after the move in, we started receiving noise complaints. One month later we received a smell complaint from the neighbor next door. When we went to investigate we noticed a strange odor coming from the young couple's condo. We knocked on their door but received no answer so we left a note stating that we would return in 24 hours to inspect the condo.

When we returned a day later, the couple was nowhere to be found so we entered their residence to find a disastrous mess. It looked as if they hadn't washed dishes in weeks! There was trash over-flowing from the trashcan, the bathtubs were soiled and the carpets were filthy. We could not believe that people would live in such a mess; the smell was horrendous. We left the couple a letter stating that we had received several complaints regarding the smell and that they would have three days to clean the condo.

A day later we received a phone call from the couple asking us to meet them in the condo parking lot. After waiting for an hour, they eventually showed up and parked their car next to us. Their car was absolutely full of junk to the point where there was no room to sit in the back seats and barely enough room to sit in the passenger seat. Looking back it was quite comical but as time passed and we interviewed more tenants, we noted a direct correlation between a messy car and a messy tenant.

When looking for quality tenants, pay special attention to their car. If it is kept in a clean condition, it is very likely that the tenant has pride of ownership and will keep your rental property in good condition.

Warning! Condo H.O.A. Fees Can Eat Up Your Cash Flow

When searching for a good cash flow property, be sure to take into consideration all the holding costs you may face. One of the costs we often see investors miscalculate is Home Owners Association (H.O.A.) fees on condominiums. This is a big mistake as these as H.O.A. fees are cash flow eaters.

H.O.A. fees are assessed for each unit based upon the square footage size. Some of the H.O.A. fees on condos we have owned ranged from $150 to $500. If you purchase a condo in a beachfront building, you will generally face higher maintenance fees due to the harsh erosion of salt water. Older condo buildings have higher H.O.A. fees as they tend to need more maintenance. All these factors should be considered when purchasing a condo unit.

Another issue to be considered is H.O.A. assessments. An assessment is a lump sum amount charged by the H.O.A. These assessments occur due to expensive building repairs and maintenance such as roof replacement or exterior painting.

In recent years, foreclosure properties have increased in volume. A consequence of excessive foreclosures is delinquent H.O.A. fees. This has become a major problem in high foreclosure states like Florida, California and Nevada. If the condo complex has a high rate of foreclosure, it is likely that the owners facing foreclosure have not been paying their H.O.A. fees. If they have not been paying their mortgage, why would they be paying their H.O.A. fees? The answer is they probably aren't.

How would this foreclosure problem affect you as an owner? H.O.A. fees have to be raised to make up for the shortfall of the delinquent owners. If only half of the owners are paying their fees, chances are the H.O.A. is running at a deficit and may be unable to pay its bills. The H.O.A. has to compensate for this deficit by increasing its monthly fees.

We have seen this situation happen with condos we owned and the situation was not pretty. It was frustrating knowing the units next to ours were occupied, but the owners were not paying their H.O.A. fees.

What is the moral of this story? Be an educated investor and plan for these potential costs. Also take into consideration that H.O.A. fees almost never go down. We have yet to see even ONE example where fees have been reduced. They *always* go up.

It is also important to remember that these fees need to be paid even when your rental unit is vacant, so make sure you calculate this into your holding costs in order to avoid a negative cash flow situation.

Not all Home Owners Associations are well run and we have seen many cases of mismanagement. Before you consider purchasing a condo unit, ask to see the accounting for the H.O.A. and educate yourself on the monthly fees, financial standing, reserve amounts and potential future assessment possibilities.

Retaining a Good Tenant Will Save You Thousands

When you come to purchase rental properties, there is one important concept you need to understand to make it a profitable business. A tenant moving out will be very hard on your wallet due to repair costs, advertising expenses and vacancy losses. It is essential you do whatever you can to keep a good tenant. Most new landlords underestimate the costs of repairing and cleaning for a new tenant. Here are some general costs you may experience during a tenant vacancy:

Interior paint:	$300
Flooring replacement:	$1300
Tile grout cleaning:	$200
Bath tile cleaning and repairs:	$150
Advertising expense:	$400
Holding costs:	$1200
General cleaning:	$150

TOTAL COST: $3700

These costs vary depending on the property and the tenant, but in every case, this expense is one you should try to avoid. By the time you calculate the costs of repairs, paint and marketing, it can eat away all your profits! Following a vacancy, it can take several weeks to find a new tenant.

If a tenant contacts you in regards to moving out, find out the issues because in certain cases, they can be resolved. We find one of the most common reasons for tenants wanting to move is their desire to purchase a home. This situation can be used to your advantage. On several occasions we have offered these tenants an opportunity to enter into a lease to buy agreement' on the home they are currently renting or have sold them another property in our inventory.

In another example a tenant was upset because his air conditioning unit was not cold enough and was prepared to move. We were able to fix his air-conditioning the following day and as an apology, installed ceiling fans in the bedrooms. Additionally, we convinced him to extend his lease by offering him a grocery store gift card.

One of our favorite tenants was almost lured away by an apartment complex that was offering three hundred dollars in cash as a 'move in special'. When we asked our tenant why she wanted to leave, she explained how important the $300 was to her. It turned out her son had been sick and she had been unable to work for two weeks. We explained to her that moving would cost much more than $300 and we offered her half a month's free in return for her extending her lease. Our tenant was thrilled! It felt good to be able to help her out and in return, we were able to retain a quality tenant who always paid rent on time and was no trouble.

Do everything in your power to keep good tenants but do not be afraid to let the troublesome ones walk if you have the opportunity. Just make sure you get everything in writing if a tenant wants to break their lease.

Here is a list of helpful ideas to retain your tenants:

Add a ceiling fan.

Offer a grocery store gift card in return for a lease extension.

Offer a half-month's rent discount to extend a lease.

For houses offer six months of free lawn care.

For houses with pools, offer six months of free pool service.

For every month they pay on time send them a $25 cash rebate.

Try to avoid offering expensive rewards, which require large out of pocket expenses for you. Monthly incentives are perfect since a tenant still might move on mid-way through their lease.

Keep in mind you will not be able to retain every good tenant. You may lose some due to new rental incentives or due to a tenant's personal or professional situation changing. Strive to retain good tenants through upgrades and incentives as these minor concessions cost far less than the expense of a vacancy.

Ex-landlord References - Beware!

One of the oldest landlord rules you will hear is to always check potential tenants' references, particularly ex-landlord references. This rule is good in theory but BEWARE! An ex-landlord may only be telling you what you want to hear.

Jim is a friend of ours who owns and manages several rental units. When he started out, Jim only owned two rental units. One was his personal rental and the other was his mother's rental.

Jim recalled a time when he interviewed a couple that was interested in renting his mother's townhouse. The couple seemed nice, however Jim made sure that he completed criminal and credit checks. He also contacted the couple's current landlord. While the couple's credit report was filled with issues, their ex-landlord gave them a glowing recommendation explaining how they were never any trouble and how they always paid their rent on time.

Ignoring the poor credit report and focusing on the glowing recommendation led Jim to sign a one-year lease with the couple. It did not take long for Jim to realize he had made a big mistake.

Within two weeks of them moving in, Jim received three phone calls from the neighbors regarding noise complaints. The couple's first rent payment was one week late and the second payment was never received. After several unsuccessful attempts to collect the rent, Jim was forced to proceed with an eviction.

After hearing this story, it was obvious the couple's previous landlord was anxious to give them a glowing recommendation in order to be rid of them. Had Jim paid attention to the other apparent warning signs, he might have thought twice about renting to this couple. Jim's story is all too common for one reason.

The first red flag should have been the poor credit report. You should not expect every potential tenant to have a flawless rental history but you will have to set your own standards as to what is acceptable. Pay special attention to such things as excessive late car payments. These types of late payments usually result in car repossessions which create work transportation problems and guess what? No work = no rent. If people cannot make their car payments on-time, do you think they will make timely rent payments? The answer is probably not. Just like the car loan company, you will probably be hunting the tenants down trying to collect your rent and that is one of the worst positions to be placed in as a landlord.

Another consideration is the mind frame of the ex-landlord. If the tenant is still living in his rental property and things are not going well, there is a VERY good chance the landlord is going to say anything to get rid of tenant.

So how do you protect yourself from being a victim of a fake landlord reference?

You should ask leading questions concerning *why* the person is moving. Moving is a huge hassle and comes with a considerable expense for all parties involved so most people do not move unless they have to. When you interview a potential tenant, ask questions such as:

- How did you make payments to your last/current landlord?

- Were your payments ever late?

- When we contact your landlord, will he tell us that you always pay rent on time?

- Why do you want to move?

If the tenant shows any hesitation in answering these questions, you should to proceed cautiously. You certainly do not want to alienate a potential tenant but you also need to be aware that some people will lie during the application process and these are usually problematic tenants.

The next step is to ask for proof of rent payments by asking for copies of three months of bank statements. This is usually the deal sealer because it shows accountability by the potential tenant. If they are unwilling to show the statements, there is usually a good reason why.

Landlord references are usually more truthful *after* the person has moved out because the landlord then has nothing to lose. Be sure to call ex-landlords, not just the current one. By making the effort to take this extra step, you will see the quality of your tenants selections improve dramatically.

Having said this, landlord references need to be taken with a grain of salt. Verify potential tenants using bank statements, credit reports, background checks, and your instincts. If your instincts are telling you something is not right, pay attention to this and you will make better decisions.

Only Accept Automatic Rent Payments

One of our rental policies states that a tenant must pay rent using an ACH - also referred to as Automated Clearing House. If you are a landlord and are not using an ACH to collect rent payments, then you are making a big mistake. Some landlords love chasing after tenants who pay their rent late because it means they can collect additional late fees. For us, our time is very valuable so collecting late rent payments is the last thing on our minds. Tenants who pay their rent late tend to be reoccurring offenders and generally live paycheck to paycheck. You might find yourself spending days (or weeks) trying to collect that extra late fee. To us, it's just not worth it.

When we interview potential tenants, we ask them if they object to being put under an automatic rental collection payment system each month. This is a great indicator of how reliable your tenants will be in regards to paying rent on time. If a potential tenant seems wary of agreeing to an automatic rent payment collection, it usually means they will be a problem tenant. On occasion, we have been lenient and rented to tenants who opposed enrolling in automatic rent collection. Each and every one of those tenants regularly paid their rent late and in some cases ended up being evicted within just a few months of moving in.

Setting up an ACH for monthly rent collection is very simple and highly effective. Only 0.5% of our tenants placed on automatic rent collection failed to meet their rent payment obligations on time; needless to say this method of rent collection is highly effective.

When you set up rent collection in this manner, it is possible a tenant will not have enough money in their bank account to meet the rent in which case you are still able to attempt to collect a late fee if this happens. As a landlord, this will free up your time spent chasing after delinquent tenants.

Another big advantage of using this payment system is that it is incontestable. Either the tenant has the money in their bank account on the day rent is due, or they don't. You will have proof whether or not the rent payment was made on time.

The following excuses will now become a thing of the past:

"The check is in the mail, you didn't get it?"

"Can I pay you cash tomorrow?"

"I forgot to mail it to you."

"I have my half but my roommate doesn't have theirs."

"My dog ate my rent check."

Are you asking yourself what the downside is? There's only one downside and it is a tiny one. You will have to pay a small fee to the automatic rent collection company for the service but the fee is nominal. Remember that time is money and the less time you spend worrying about rent collection, the more real estate deals you can be searching for.

Our preferred company for automatic rent collection is Clear Now.

We have set up a special offer for a reader where you receive two months FREE service with Clear Now.

Visit www.clearnow.com/?part=51 or www.101rules.com/tools for more information.

Always Have Written Procedures and Policies in Place and Have Your Tenants Sign Them

Some tenants will use every trick in the book to their advantage and unfortunately, most laws favor the tenant and not the landlord. Because of this fact, you must make sure you are covered should any issues arrive.

We once rented a small single family home to a man named George, his wife Alisa and their two small children. George had recently moved from Mexico but had a relatively good comprehension of the English language. Alisa however spoke very little English. During the tenant interview, we explained our rental policies and procedures to them both.

We always keep our rules, policies and procedures in writing and have tenants sign them so if there are any issues, everything is in plain writing. We explained to George that in order to rent from us, he would need to read our policies and sign them, to which he happily agreed.

Several issue-free months passed but then George started to become late on his rent payments. We try to work with all of our tenants if they are having difficulty paying the rent, but George was not communicating with us. In fact he appeared to be completely avoiding us.

Our phone calls went unanswered for 10 days and messages requesting call backs were ignored. We felt as if the inevitable eviction was looming in George's future. Evictions are things we try to avoid but when running a rental business but sometimes we have no other choice as you cannot let people live in your rentals for free.

As we were heading to the courthouse to file eviction papers we received a phone call from George. He explained he had been sick and that he wanted to talk to us about his rent situation. We met with George later that day and were quite surprised when he explained that he did not understand the rent payment procedures. George told us he had thought that the rent was far less expensive than what he was paying and that he wanted us to reduce the rent amount. We explained to George that he had read and signed our rental policy and procedures which explained quite clearly the rent amounts and when it was due. We did not mention the fact he had been paying the correct amount of rent for several months

George argued that he had not understood what he was signing and he thought the rent was too high. He gave as an ultimatum: either we reduce the rent or he would take us to court. We advised George that going to court would be a waste of his time and money. Since he had clearly signed the rental policies and procedures agreement and the lease, we knew he had no case. George continued to argue with us and our conversation was going nowhere quickly. We explained to him that if he felt going to court applicable, he should proceed forward as we would be continuing our eviction since his rent had not been paid in over 10 days.

We gave George every opportunity to catch up with his rent but it seemed as if he wanted to live in our property for as long as possible for free. This was a situation we had been warned about by other landlords and was one of the main reasons why we had tenants sign the policies and procedures agreement. We left George's house that day feeling uneasy about what was to follow as we felt George was trying to scam us. Several days later we received an attorney's letter in the mail stating George was suing us for misleading him, claiming we *forced* him to sign a rental agreement he did not understand. We knew George had little chance of winning such a lawsuit but it still proved to be inconvenient as he was still living in our home rent-free.

There was little else we could do but to wait for a court date and hope the judge would rule in our favor. We finally received the court date and gathered all of our documents to present to the judge. We provided the signed lease and the policy and procedures agreement which clearly stated the rent and deposit amounts. The judge reviewed the documents and asked George what proof he had that we had misled him - of course he had none. It was his word against our documents, which resulted in George losing the case and having to pay back rent and both our court fees and attorneys costs.

Keeping good records and making sure your documents are organized is essential to being a successful landlord. If we had not written out our policies and procedures we might have lost that court case resulting in weeks of loss rent and thousands of dollars in out of pocket attorney and court fees. Thankfully we won the case and were able to proceed forward with the eviction process.

Always make sure your tenants sign a policies and procedures agreement in their own handwriting, that way it is very difficult for them to argue that they did not understand what they were signing. Their signature is binding and can make the difference between winning and losing a court case. Unfortunately, these situations do happen from time to time so it is best to be prepared!

For more information about policies and procedures and agreements visit www.101rules.com/tools

The Once A Month Inspection Is the Secret to Keeping Tenants in Line

Generally, the most consistent rule about tenants is that they care little about your property due to a lack of 'pride of ownership.' Renters will take care of their own belongings better than they will take care of yours. It's just the way it is in the landlord world and you have to learn not to take it personally.

We once rented a small two-bedroom two-bathroom house to a woman named Michelle. During the tenant interview she seemed like a nice person and her appearance was neat and tidy. We soon found out that looks can be deceiving. After three months of very little communication with Michelle, we decided to stop by the house to make sure she was settling in well and to see if she needed anything.

We tend to keep a supply of air conditioning filters in our car as sometimes the tenants forget to change them so we do it for them. We called and left Michelle a message letting her know that we would be stopping by two days later. She did not return our phone call so we decided to stop by anyways. Legally we are required to give a tenant 24 hours notice before a visit so we made sure we were well within this timeframe.

After knocking and ringing the doorbell for several minutes, it seemed that Michelle was not at home so we decided to enter the home and change the air conditioning filter. When we opened the door we were horrified to see a disastrous mess. There were half eaten cans of food on the floor with ants crawling inside them, dirty laundry on the couch and cat feces in the kitchen. Michelle's home smelled like an overloaded five day old trash can on a hot summer's day. We immediately called and told her as per the rental agreement, she was required to keep her home clean and that this situation needed to be taken care of immediately.

Michelle called us back immediately and was very apologetic and embarrassed explaining that she normally wouldn't live that way. It turned out that Michelle had run into some financial difficulties and was forced to take double shifts at work seven days a week, leaving her little time for anything else other than eating and sleeping. Michelle true to her word cleaned the house and kept it in good order for the rest of her time there.

From that day on we made it a habit of visiting each of our rental properties once a month to change the act conditioning filters, and spray for pests. We found that once the tenants knew we would be visiting on a regular basis, they took much better care of their residences, which was beneficial for all concerned parties.

Do Not Be Afraid To Evict When It Is Necessary

Evictions are a painful but necessary part of being a successful landlord. Let's face it, no one likes to evict or to be evicted however if your tenant is causing you problems, sometimes it is the only solution.

During our weekly viewing of the county real estate auction list, we noticed a house that was of particular interest. The house was a two-bedroom, two-bathroom, single family home located close to the interstate, making it attractive for work commuters.

We decided to set a low target price and bid on this property. When we arrived at the auction there was a room full of people, however only a handful were there to bid. Thankfully, few of them were interested in the same house that we wanted, leading us to be successful in our bidding attempt.

The following day we traveled to our newly acquired house, knocked on the door and we were greeted by a gentleman named Chuck. Sometimes when we buy homes from auctions there is still a tenant living in them, unaware of the sale. This was the case here.

When Chuck opened the door, an unpleasant smell wafted outside and into our nostrils. Chuck smelt as if he had not taken a bath in a month, so we feared the worst in regards to the interior of the house. Chuck was reluctant to let us in and insisted we show him proof of ownership since he was unaware the property had been sold at auction. Since we did not have the deed to the house with us we were unable to persuade him that we were the new owners.

Even though Chuck would not let us inside the house, we could see that the interior was in disrepair and could tell he was a hoarder. There were numerous boxes stored all around the living room and on the couch. Chuck told us he had been renting this property from his ex-wife for five years and he was in no mood to move. From that conversation we knew he was going to be an issue so we said our goodbyes and considered ways in which to handle this delicate situation.

We really only had two options:

1.   Maintain Chuck as a tenant.
2.   Ask him to leave or evict if necessary.

Since this situation occurred early in our real estate careers, we had minimal experience dealing with tenants. We decided it was in our best interests to keep things peaceful and try to maintain Chuck as a tenant. Looking back, this was a big mistake as Chuck did not own a telephone so right from the beginning, we were always chasing after him.

The second time we drove to the house we offered Chuck a rent reduction in return for him maintaining the property and completing some simple repairs such as cleaning up the house, painting and drywall patching. Chuck happily agreed to this and we informed him that he would need to sign a new one-year lease within the next 24 hours.

Twenty-four hours later when we drove back to the house at the agreed time and knocked on the door, Chuck was nowhere to be found. We tried again the following day but again, no Chuck. We were becoming irritated as the house was a 40 minute drive from where we lived. We left a note on Chuck's door explaining that if he did not call us within the next three days our agreed rental deal would be terminated. We hoped for the best but we knew this situation was not looking good and as expected, no phone call was received from Chuck. Thus, we had no choice but to go forward with the eviction process.

Three days after beginning the eviction process we received a phone call from Chuck saying that he had been out of town and that he would still like to go ahead with the rental agreement. He also said he would be working for the next three days and for us to come by on the weekend. We decided it would be easier to try to working out the agreement rather than going through the eviction process and having to find a new tenant.

Three days later, we drove back to the house and knocked on the door. Chuck again was nowhere to be found. We waited for an hour to see if he would return but he did not. It was becoming apparent that Chuck was using delaying tactics so he could live in the house rent free for as long as possible. Now was definitely time to evict as Chuck had delayed us for almost three weeks and cost us $900 in rental income, not to mention the hours spent driving back and forth to the house.

This experience taught us good lessons on knowing when to listen to your gut instincts and cut your losses. If you find yourself in a similar situation, know when the time has come to evict so you do not face the same delays that we did. Never try to sugarcoat the truth because you will end up deceiving yourself that can be very costly.

PROFESSIONALISM

Home Offices Can Destroy Productivity

When we started our real estate company, we really hit the ground running. We profitably flipped our first house and never slowed down. Our heavy workloads made our lives both hectic and exciting. Our business involved managing repairs, contractors, marketing, promoting, and printing etc. etc.

During the early years we worked out of a home office in order to keep our monthly expenses down to a minimum. Working out of a home office involves many distractions such as pets, spouses, kids, Internet, and chores. These distractions can instantly eat up your productivity. We have first handedly experienced how these seemingly small distractions hugely impacted our ability to complete tasks in a timely manner.

After a few years of completing many successful real estate deals, we decided to share our knowledge and wrote our first book, 'Real Estate Tax Deed Investing: How We Made Over $1,000,000 in Two Years!' We wanted to share our success stories and watch others grow and achieve their life goals. Over the years, we have found many experienced investors that were not willing to share their secrets or wanted people to pay thousands of dollars to attend useless seminars. Being experts in the field, we decided it was time to change that practice and offer the same advice for the low price of a book.

We began the long and arduous process of book writing but after four months, we found ourselves distracted daily. It was not writer's block or laziness but more a lack of focus. We had set ourselves a four-month goal of completion and it was frustrating that we could not achieve this goal. We tried locking ourselves inside our office and setting deadlines but nothing seemed to work. We just could not meet our four-month goal and it was looking as if we would have trouble meeting a one year completion deadline. Something had to change, but what?

In the midst of our book-writing project, a prominent Orlando criminal attorney approached us to partner with him on a huge land deal he was in the process of assembling. This attorney was well versed in real estate deals and was very forward thinking so the opportunity of working with him excited us.

Since the deal was so large and the attorney wanted us to work hand in hand with him, he provided us with some unused office space. The office was not much larger than an average dining room but it was big enough for two desks, computers and filing cabinets - exactly what we needed.

We set a schedule for ourselves, which involved arriving in the office daily by a certain time, and within the first week, our productivity skyrocketed. Not only were we accomplishing bigger real estate deals, our book content flowed and the writing became easier and easier. Our small office became lovingly known as the 'War Room'.

As our focus sharpened, all the typical everyday distractions we faced in our home office were eliminated. Even though we still have home offices, we regularly use our business office, especially when we need to knuckle down and be extra productive! The price we pay for the office pales in comparison to the high work levels we achieve there. This type of productivity is priceless to us.

If you find yourself being distracted as we were, a change of scenery can work wonders. Find an office where you can be around like-minded people who help each other grow. Solutions such as community offices can include a communal secretary and other amenities that would otherwise be costly. These offices are a gathering place to nourish new ideas and build great relationships. Many of our friendships and business relationships were formed due to our new office, relationships that we still cherish today.

When you share an office with like-minded individuals, your productivity will grow along with your resources and connections. You will be involved in the action rather than being on the outside. Keep this in mind while searching for your new War Room!

Failing to Plan Is Planning to Fail

Real estate investing can be overwhelming if you are unprepared. By purchasing this book you have shown you are ready to take the next step to becoming a successful real estate investor. Now it is time to get organized!

On any given day our 'to do' list can be extensive. Organizing these lists enables us to manage even the most difficult renovation projects, ensuring that they became profitable ventures.

For example, when tackling a renovation project, start with a basic list and try to outline every aspect. Begin by walking through the property noting down *everything* that needs to be repaired... roof, paint, carpet, closets, doorknobs, and appliances... everything. Following that, you can input all the repairs into a spreadsheet or use online project management software such as Project Bubble.

We have negotiated a special offer with Project Bubble so sign up for your free trial by visiting www.101rules.com/tools or directly at http://goo.gl/ xpn6q

After you have inputted your 'to do' list, organize by importance.

Lack of organization has been the downfall of many real estate investors we have met. Using our suggested methods will leave you nicely organized and give you more time to focus on the tasks at hand.

We have found that some beginner investors become overwhelmed by the sheer number of tasks that need to be completed during a renovation project. Project Bubble is a great tool to keep these tasks organized. To be a successful real estate investor you must identify, assign, complete, and follow up.

With two of us working on multiple projects we never assume anything. Strict delegation of repairs and tasks is essential to complete a project on time and within budget.

Increase Your Business through Professional and Inviting Communication

With the advancement in technology, some forms of communication have become rather impersonal, particularly text messages and emails. The telephone however offers you the opportunity to make a good first impression. Those first impressions can set the foundation for your future relationships. In the world of real estate and business, there is no second chance at making a good first impression.

You probably don't give much thought to your communication style and techniques. When your phone rings, you can either answer or send the caller to voice mail. This is a simple choice. When you receive an email, you can reply immediately, later, or not at all. Again, simple choices but keep in mind when you are first contacted or introduced to someone new, your choice in the way you respond can leave a lasting impression, good or bad.

For example we once had a fantastic three-bedroom, two-bathroom house for sale located on a lake in a quiet neighborhood. There were very few houses for sale in this area so we had quite a gem on our hands.

We did not use an agent for this property because it was located close to a major road so our road signs generated drive-by traffic. The first day we put out our signs, we received phone calls from interested people. Thinking nothing of it we answered the phones the way we always do.... by simply saying "Hello."

A real estate agent called and the conversation went something like this:

Matt: "Hello?"

Jerry: "I'm sorry I hope I dialed the right number. I was looking for the person selling the three-bedroom, two-bath house near Curry Woods... is that you?"

Matt: "You've got him."

Jerry: "Oh, ok, well I was interested in viewing the property with a client of mine…"

We were confused by the "I'm sorry I hope I dialed the right number" comment because we were thinking… "Of course this is the person selling the house, you called the number listed on the sign!"

After the phone call ended and a viewing appointment had been arranged, we discussed the comment Jerry had made about dialing the right number. We concluded that answering that first phone call was a stepping stone to selling the property and that every word that came out of our mouths was setting the stage for the future relationship. How we answered the phone call was just as important as the rest of the call.

The next day, we called Jerry one hour before his appointment to confirm he would be arriving on time. Jerry answered after two rings:

"Hello, this is Jerry with Coldwell Banker, how can I help you?"

Jerry's professional communication style and tone made a lasting impression on us. After speaking with him for a few minutes, we knew he was a person we wanted to do business with.

We met Jerry and his client later that day and they made us an offer on the lakefront house. 45 days later we closed on the property.

You may be thinking that this is all common sense. We would agree but thinking back to our first conversation with Jerry we realized how badly we had missed the mark with our communication. Sometimes we find people to be very impersonal on the phone and act as if *we* are inconveniencing or interrupting them! The first time you come into contact with someone, how you greet them will set the foundation for your relationship moving forward.

The more we considered our communication style, the more we realized improvement was needed. We immediately changed our phone greeting to: "Hello, this is Matt / Laurence, how can I help you today?" If we have multiple properties for sale and we are being flooded with phone calls, we will answer, "Hello this is Matt/ Laurence, which property are you calling about today?"

Our investor friend Matt laughed when we told him we were writing a whole chapter on the importance of phone greetings within the real estate field. Two days later we met Matt for lunch and when we went to pick up the bill, Matt snatched it from the table and refused to allow us to pay. He apologized for laughing at our chapter idea and explained that after our conversation, he became consciously aware of how others answered the phone. Matt was enlightened by how peoples' phone communication styles directly related to their professionalism, reliability and accountability.

Matt went on to explain that his handyman who worked slowly and was constantly late always answered the phone with a simple "Hello." Matt's landscaper (who was always reliable and on time), answered his phone far more professionally and returned calls in a timely manner.

Matt had failed to see this correlation and explained that the more he communicated with his workers, the more he spotted this trend. It was really an eye opener for him. Not only does Matt pay far greater attention to the way he answers and communicates on the phone, he uses this rule to make better decisions about people.

Our rule relates to email and voicemail as well. There may be times where you have to conduct business via text message or email before ever meeting a person face to face. Use those opportunities to improve your communication techniques. Think about how those emails will be portrayed and what you would think of them if you were the receiver rather than the sender.

Be watchful as to how people you do business with handle your calls, and emails. How long does it take for them to reply? Are they returning your calls within a 24 hour time period?

When you call a plumbing company do they answer the phone, "Hello?", or do they answer: "Bob's Plumbing, this is Bob. How can I help you?" Even though you are only a few seconds into the conversation, you should be considering these small tell tale signs or professionalism. The advice given within the 'Increase Your Business through Professional and Inviting Communication' rule is intended to have a positive impact on you and your business. It will teach you to avoid the mistakes we made. Some of the suggestions may seem minor however we assure you they will have a positive long-term impact on you and your business relationships.

Keep a Daily Log of Phone Calls, Conversations, Deadlines, and Commitments

Disagreements happen often, especially when it comes to contractors, subcontractors, and laborers. Many of these disagreements can be avoided by keeping good records. Depending on your preference of communication, your level of documentation will vary. Obviously it's hard to document something that is said during a phone call so we prefer to use text messaging and emails for confirmations, that way we have written proof.

If we do make verbal plans, we still document what is said and agreed upon. This is very important when we ask a painter to arrive at 7 a.m. and they do not show up until 9 a.m. *We need to document these conversations so all parties involved are held accountable.*

On one occasion we spoke with a drywall subcontractor and made arrangements for him to complete three apartments we were renovating. We reiterated the importance of him being on time, due to us having the apartments under sales contracts with unchangeable closing deadlines. Unfortunately the drywall contractor forgot the start date and the morning he was supposed to start the job, he was nowhere to be found. When we finally contacted him a day later, he informed us he was on another job and thought our start date was two weeks later. It took us almost five days to find an alternative drywall contractor, which ultimately put us four days behind our sales contract dates and resulted in us losing those contracts. This mistake cost us thousands of dollars in holding costs but taught us the valuable lesson of getting everything in writing. When working with a contractor, insist on putting everything in writing to avoid the costly mistakes we made. If you cannot get something in writing, use a notebook to document as much as you can. Communicate with emails and always keep copies. Since emails require such a small amount of space on your computer, record each project in an individual file and keep the files indefinitely in case future disputes arise.

Respond to Phone Calls and Emails Promptly

In an industry where time is literally money, whether in the form of loan interest, payroll, or property holding costs, everyone's time is valuable.

Demand the respect you deserve by insisting your contractors return your phone calls and emails within a 24-hour time period. When ending a phone conversation that requires a delayed response say, "So I can expect a call back by tomorrow before what time?" This committal will expose your contractor's true values and may be a good indication of how prompt he will be appearing on your job site.

Make sure to show these contractors (and other people you do business with) the same respect you wish to receive. If you promise to return a phone call at a certain time, follow through to the best of your ability. The same goes for attending meetings and arriving on time; the people you do business with will be appreciative and it will encourage them to act in a similar manner.

When dealing with real estate transactions and doing business with many individuals, good communication is the key. There is nothing more frustrating than leaving a message or sending an email that is not replied to within a reasonable time period.

We have rejected many bids from real estate professionals simply because they have returned our phone calls within reasonable time. It still amazes us how we can call 10 painters and are lucky if two call back within 24 hours. Some *never* return the call!

We hear people offer excuses for such actions such as "They must not need the work". That is utter nonsense because in our experience, the contractors who do not return phone calls are the ones who need the work the most as they are often just lazy, forgetful and bad business people.

Do not be a bad business person. Always return phone calls as soon as you can and request others do the same for you.

Never Assume Anything

No matter what trade you are working with – Real estate agents, painters, GCs, architects, plumbers, etc. – never assume anything!

There are no stupid questions so ask away. For instance: Let's say you ordered a pedestal sink with a black faucet. Ask if other installation parts are included such as piping. Many people would assume this to be so but sometimes these parts come at an additional cost so you should always ask and never assume.

When you sell a property you generally need a survey. Check to make sure this is completed as it will not always be taken care of for you.

When a contractor tells you he will be there "in the morning," is his morning 7.00 a.m. or 11.59 a.m.? Do not assume you know the answer and have the contractor commit to a specific time. 'Morning' alone is unacceptable.

Always ask detailed questions and leave no stone unturned. If there are unanswered questions concerning who is responsible for what, then ask. It is so much easier to address details so everyone is on the same page than to ignore them and have things go awry. It still amazes us how things we assume as common sense are often missed by others and vice versa.

Your painting contractor may assume you are providing all the paint and he just has to apply it. You may assume he is providing the paint. He may assume you only require two colors: the base and the trim. You may assume the quote includes multiple colors or specific brands of paint. See how this works? Ask - it will avoid many problems.

In our earlier story involving José the painter, he assumed we would provide all the supplies while we assumed he would be bringing his own equipment and supplies. This situation could have been easily avoided through better communication. Avoid the mistakes we made by never assuming anything!

Acknowledge Your Mistakes and Take Action to Fix Them

Mistakes happen - you are only human. Everyone makes mistakes during their real estate careers (including your business partners). As long as you acknowledge, learn from and try not to repeat these mistakes, it is acceptable to make them. For us, we find ways to turn mistakes into learning experiences. Mistakes happen for many reasons: lack of information, haste, ego, or the inability to make decisions.

You will not experience the joy from success if you've never experienced the disappointment of failure. Acknowledge your mistakes and learn from them. Most importantly, if you can avoid repeating your mistakes, you will be well ahead of the game.

For example, when we purchased our first rental condo, we seemed to have trouble renting to good quality tenants who paid on time. We learned (after two evictions) that the problem was not the tenants… it was us! *WE* were the ones selecting and agreeing to rent to the tenants so we had to take responsibility.

We soon learned from our mistakes and made some adjustments.

- We performed better tenant screening and background checks.

- We checked all references including those from ex-landlords.

- We set up automatic bank withdrawals for rent payments.

- We acted quickly when problems arose instead of ignoring them.

- We learned to be patient and waited for better quality tenants.

The more we learned from our mistakes, the better real estate investors and human beings we became. We now ignore the 'Just get a tenant in there so we can start collecting rent!' feeling that accompanies being a landlord. Today, far less problems arise as a result.

Matt's Rule: Know When to Dress the Part and When to Dress Down

I am the first one to admit that I love nothing more than to relax in shorts and a tank top! It took me YEARS of listening to my business partner harping on that it was unprofessional before I got the message (I hate it when he's right!).

In one instance, we were shopping for a large loan on a piece of land we had under contract. After weeks of shopping, we found a bank offering an affordable interest rate. All we needed was a face-to-face meeting with the bank's loan manager. I did not think twice about my attire and dressed very casually for the meeting. The loan manager sat down at the meeting but never took me seriously and consequently, we were denied the loan and lost the contract on the land. This was a painful lesson learned and now I always dress appropriately.

The experience with the loan manager was a large wake up call for me to stop being so stubborn and hypocritical. I realized that public perception is (unfortunately) more important to most people than reality! There was a line for me to draw and while I was not about to spend $3000 on a wristwatch, I did update my wardrobe.

The more I associated with business professionals, the more I realized how important my attire was. I had resisted change for so long because I felt it encroached on my personality and honestly, I didn't feel comfortable in a suit and tie. As time passed, I found myself judging people in certain situations whom I thought were under-dressed, so I decided people must have been doing the same to me. Nice jeans and pants replaced the shorts, a dress shirt replaced the printed t-shirts and the ever present five 'o'clock shadow was tackled daily with a sharp razor. Honestly, I wasn't over thrilled about the dress changes at first but as time passed, presenting a professional persona became increasingly important to me. I soon realized my actions reflected strongly upon my business partner and others I worked with. Dressing appropriately for the occasion is now at the forefront of my mind at all times.

Give To Charities

Eighty-hour work weeks were a normal occurrence for us when we started in real estate. Countless weeks were spent researching and driving around viewing *hundreds* of properties, searching for the right deal. After we acquired a new property, we spent weeks and sometimes months repairing and marketing it to ensure we made a profit. At times it was not easy but we persisted.

When you work for yourself you never quite know what income you will be producing from week to week, so for us it was difficult to grasp the concept of giving to charity. We were always afraid of running out of money so donating to a cause seemed unrealistic. Every penny we earned was reinvested into another real estate deal.

One day while searching for some staging equipment, our charitable giving views changed. We had purchased several homes in a retirement community located in Mount Dora, Florida. Mount Dora is filled with many gorgeous golf courses and considered a golfers' heaven. One day we decided to take a few hours off work and hit the links for nine holes of hacking. After each losing a dozen balls on the first six holes, we received a phone call from a local real estate agent who knew we were looking for a couple of pieces of furniture to place in a vacant home for staging purposes. The agent gave us the phone number of a woman named Sharron whom we called and set up a meeting with.

When we arrived at her house, her husband Todd greeted us and proceeded to show us all their staging supplies. They owned beds, mirrors, dressers, tables, cups, dishes, candles; it was apparent they had enough supplies to furnish at least three homes. While all of this furniture was nice, we really only needed a few items.

After browsing the items for half an hour, Sharron came outside to meet us. She was in her late 50's and bursting with life. As we talked, Sharron explained that she owned a staging company but had recently been diagnosed with cancer. Sharron showed us all the items she had lovingly handpicked from stores and garage sales. Her favorite piece was ladybug cookie jar. Sharron's passion for decorating showed as she described each piece as if it belonged in her own home.

We spent some time with the couple and after sharing some stories back and forth, Sharron explained she was feeling tired and excused herself. Her husband Todd turned to us and asked us if we would consider purchasing *all* the staging equipment. He explained how Sharron loved helping her friends' stage their houses but how all the staging supplies were sitting idle, cluttering up their garage as neither one of them had the energy to run the business anymore. Todd also explained how Sharron's medical bills had become costly and how they needed money to pay for future treatment. It was a sad story indeed.

We asked Todd how much he wanted for all the staging supplies to which he responded with a number that was far below what we thought was fair. Even though cash was tight for us, we decided to offer Todd more money than he had asked for. At the time we did not really need all of these staging supplies but we knew this money would help Todd and Sharron and felt it was the right thing to do. When we told Todd we couldn't take the staging supplies for his price and wrote down our price, he was both shocked and delighted. We will never forget the look on his face.

We started loading up the equipment and called a friend with a larger vehicle to come pick up the remaining items. As we were loading, Todd approached us and explained that Sharron's cancer was progressing rapidly and asked if we would object to him donating our money to a cancer research charity. We agreed to Todd's request and wrote him an additional check so they would have enough money to help with their medical bills and donate to the American Cancer Society. Todd was thrilled. As we pulled out the driveway, Sharron came out to say goodbye. Todd had told her about our donation gesture and she was in tears, thanking us over and over. It was an emotional moment that we will never forget. We knew we had made the right decision and it felt good to help someone in need. It also felt good knowing our donation might help others in the future.

Several months later we received a call from a couple in the Mount Dora area asking if we had staging equipment to rent. This was bizarre because we did not usually stage other people's properties.

We later found out that this couple was a friend of Sharron's. They had called Todd to rent staging furniture and he explained to them what we had done for Sharron. The couple wanted to help us by renting our staging supplies instead of using another company. We were grateful for Todd's recommendation since most of our new staging supplies were not being used.

After agreeing on terms, we visited the couple's house and saw it was in perfect condition. We all worked together to place the staging items and after we had finished, the house looked like a model home. Our staging services were only needed for three months but the couple paid us for an extra two months as a bonus since they were thrilled to have sold their house so quickly.

When we arrived at the couple's house to pick up our staging furniture, we learned the sad news that Sharron had passed away shortly after we had met her. This was a very sad day.

The next time you have an opportunity to help someone, whether it is by donating your time or your money, we encourage you to do so. Helping Sharron was a life-changing event for us, and now we donate to good causes whenever we can.

When people ask us what our favorite staging piece is, we tell them it is Sharron's ladybug cookie jar. We still keep this jar in our houses today and it reminds us how lucky we were to have met Sharron and Todd.

When Making New Real Estate Contacts, Listen More Than You Talk

We learn new things every day since we work in an industry where nothing stays constant - it's exciting! By reading this book you set out on a journey to learn something new and you should commend yourself for that. Some of these chapters will be eye opening while others may teach you new things about a topic you already had some prior knowledge of. The key is to absorb as much information as possible and then apply it. Keeping your ears wide open is the key as we find newer investors sometimes forget to listen.

We once had a lunch meeting with a real estate investor from Miami named Javier who held an impressive investment portfolio worth $10 million. We had just broken our $1 million mark and we were excited about meeting someone so successful. During our lunch, we swapped stories of real estate deals, successes and failures. It was a very encouraging conversation.

The following day we returned home and met our agent Pat. We told him about the meeting and shared some of Javier's stories. Pat said, "Sounds like a fun meeting but what did you two learn?"

We looked at each other for a second and realized we had been so excited about sharing our experiences that we hadn't really paid attention to what Javier had told us. In other words, we were present, but not really listening. There is nothing wrong with story swapping but in this case we had missed out on a huge opportunity to learn from a highly experienced investor. We felt somewhat foolish.

Fortunately this question of "What did you learn?" has stuck with us. We were fortunate to meet Javier two weeks later and the conversation went in a new direction. We used the meeting time to listen and be present as Javier shared his experience and knowledge. By focusing the conversation on Javier instead of on ourselves, we were able to learn valuable information that in the future helped grow our real estate business.

Go To a City and County Government Meeting and Get Involved

Government meetings used to interest us about as much as sticking our feet into a red anthill - in other words, not at all. We used to think these meetings were useless and downright boring. That all changed one day when we were driving past a large parcel of land that had a planning notice posted on it. We decided to stop and read the notice, which contained information for a zoning change application. The land owner was requesting a zoning change that would allow building over three stories to be built, an unusual request since the land was located in a residential area.

After researching the notice but finding very little information, we decided to attend the zoning public hearing. At the hearing we were disturbed to learn that the school board was attempting to build and relocate an 'F' rated high school less than 1 mile from our new residential building project. The school rebuild would feature three-story buildings in an area that contained one-story buildings. We, along with several hundred other people, were quite upset by this news and we all decided to get involved.

Although we knew there was little chance of swaying the city's decision to allow the rezoning, we felt the urge to try regardless. We knew this relocation would negatively affect the value of our land development and also our own personal residences, which were very close by. Unfortunately 'F' rated schools dramatically decrease property values and we certainly did not want this to happen.

We attended every city meeting and educated ourselves on the pros and cons of the school relocation. There was no question that a new high school was needed, however moving the school away from its current community location was not the best plan. During our research we learned that several years prior, the city had added a half-cent sales tax to pay for renovating the existing school buildings. Instead of the money being used to renovate, it was used to purchase the large of parcel land for the relocation. We also discovered that the land was purchased from a family member of one of the school board administrators.

Relocating the school would also mean many students who currently walked to school would be forced to take buses meaning added traffic and transportation costs. Many of the residents whose single lane road would be used for school bus transportation were furious.

Everyone agreed that this deal stunk of government misspending and that we would fight for the renovation of the existing school buildings since it was the most cost effective and practical solution.

We continued to attend each city meeting for the next 18 months and we were very outspoken. Our group was regularly featured on the local news and our plight became a talking point. Even some of the schoolteachers agreed with our stance.

Eventually the issue came to a vote and due to the public concerns regarding the school relocation, it was denied by a slim margin. The city decided the school should be rebuilt in its current location since the school had been there for 20 years and it was a community feature.

We were ecstatic about this decision and if we had not attended those meetings, who knows if this vote would have turned out the way it did. It is easy to think, "I cannot make a difference", but take it from us, attend city meetings and get involved. You will be surprised the difference you *can* make in your community.

Find a Mentor

We have been members of a local real estate investors club for many years and it is something we highly recommend joining. You can meet many different types of people who will inspire you and provide you with new ideas.

We once attended a club meeting that was hosted by a prominent real estate investor named Frank McKinney. Frank was well known for building exclusive South Florida mansions that were priced in the millions; he even developed a mansion priced at over $100,000,000. Frank was a very experienced homebuilder who had a vibrant and eclectic personality.

The reason Frank hosted the investors club meeting was to raise money for his foundation. Frank's passion in life is charity work. His company funds a project named 'The Caring House Project' which is devoted to providing shelter to desperately poor and homeless people in Haiti. This foundation also provides emergency relief to people in the United States through its 'Survival to Thrive on an Initiative' campaign. Frank's foundation does truly amazing work.

It costs Frank's foundation $5000 to build one home in Haiti which accommodates a homeless family. For a donation of one home, Frank offered an opportunity to visit his tree-house office for lunch and spend the afternoon touring his oceanfront construction projects. We jumped at the chance to partake in such a unique opportunity and donated to Frank's cause. The afternoon we spent with him was one of the most memorable experiences of our real estate careers. We saw the most inspiring real estate and were able to pick Frank's brain for several hours. He gave us many good tips and eventually became a mentor to us. Frank's moral character is undeniably pure and his willingness to help others expecting nothing in return is nothing short of remarkable. It is vital that you find a real estate mentor to help guide you through your real estate career. There are plenty of giving people out there like Frank who are happy to help. For more information on Frank's cause please visit www.frank-mckinney.com

Perseverance Is The Key To Success!

"The brick walls are there for a reason. The brick walls are not there to keep us out. The brick walls are there to give us a chance to show how badly we want something because the brick walls are there to stop the people who don't want it badly enough."

-Randy Pausch.

Real estate investing demands 100% perseverance. There are times when deals will fall into your lap and times when deals are non-existent for long periods of time. These droughts can last for months but you have to be persistent. Do not despair – do not give up!

An investor couple named Clay and Marie once experienced such a drought. Clay decided to search for real estate deals while keeping his regular day job as a mortgage broker. Clay thought he could increase his income by renovating one or two properties per year while offering mortgages to potential buyers. The two businesses would work well together. It had always been Clay's dream to renovate houses for a living as he enjoyed completing handyman projects in his own home. Clay had written loans for real estate investors and watched them buy, fix, sell, and profit. Clay thought he could do the same with ease.

Clay and his real estate agent searched for eight months but were unable to find a favorable deal. They placed multiple offers on houses but none were accepted. Clay eventually became disheartened and his searches became less and less frequent.

Eventually he ceased to search at all.

Marie had watched Clay struggle for the eight months and was sad to see he him give up on his dream. Marie offered to help but raising three small children and working part time consumed her life.

One day, Marie was terminated from her job position when her company closed due to the bad economy. Since Marie had extra time on her hands, she decided to drive around looking for real estate deals. She learned what to look for and was diligent in her research. After four weeks of searching, Marie discovered a potential deal only a mile away from her home.

When Marie told Clay the news, she saw his face light up with enthusiasm. However, Clay was somewhat skeptical as he had been in this position many times before. In truth, he was not sure he could stomach another rejected offer. Despite Clay's skepticism, Marie persuaded him to let her submit an offer. Five weeks later, Clay and Marie closed on their first investment property. They began working on the house in their spare time and experienced a new lease of life as they embarked on their new business venture together.

If Marie had given up searching as Clay had done, they would never have found their first real estate deal.

Searching for real estate deals may seem daunting at times but remember: if it were easy, everyone would be doing it. Persevere through the droughts and eventually deals will rain down on you.

About the Authors

Matt Merdian initially began his investment experience working with stocks, bonds, and options in Denver Colorado. After working with firms such as Oppenheimer Funds and American Express Financial Advisors, Matt moved to trade a multimillion dollar hedge fund under world renowned day trader and author David Nassar.

Laurence Samuels is a British immigrant who spent many years working in the music business as an A&R Director and musical performer before embarking on a real estate investing career.

In 2001, a relocation to Orlando, Florida turned Matt's focus to real estate investing. Matt and Laurence formed London Meridian International in 2003 buying and selling their first Tax Deed property making over $45,000. Matt and Laurence authored *Real Estate Tax Deed Investing, How we made over One Million Dollars in Two Years,* an account of their years of experience and their guide to purchasing Tax Deed properties.

Matt and Laurence now offer personalized real estate investing coaching; visit www.101Rules.com for more information. In 2012 Matt formed Wholesale Premium Properties and manages the liquidation division of Magnolia Advisors for Tax Deeds. The firm currently places tens of millions of dollars in tax liens and tax deeds each year. Laurence also owns Broadstone Media, a marketing and website design agency.

VISIT

WWW.101RULES.COM

WWW.101RULES.COM

RECOMMENDED FORMS

WWW.101RULES.COM

RENTAL DOCUMENTS

&

TOOLS

WWW.101RULES.COM

FREE

DOWNLOAD

As a thank you for purchasing this book we invite you to visit our website www.101rules.com where you will find endless resources to help you achieve your business goals and dreams.

Also Available: Real Estate and Tax Deed Deed Investing

All the information you need to become a successful real estate real estate investor!

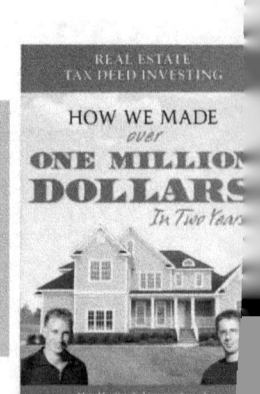

REAL ESTATE
TAX DEED INVESTING

HOW WE MADE *over*
ONE MILLION DOLLARS *In Two Years*

www.ingramcontent.com/pod-product-compliance
Lightning Source LLC
Chambersburg PA
CBHW071426170526
45165CB00001B/414